SAVE
YOURSELF

SAVE YOURSELF

CAMERON ESPOSITO

GRAND CENTRAL
PUBLISHING

NEW YORK   BOSTON

Grand Central Publishing
Hachette Book Group
1290 Avenue of the Americas, New York, NY 10104
grandcentralpublishing.com
twitter.com/grandcentralpub

First Edition: March 2020

Grand Central Publishing is a division of Hachette Book Group, Inc. The Grand Central Publishing name and logo is a trademark of Hachette Book Group, Inc.

The publisher is not responsible for websites (or their content) that are not owned by the publisher.

Library of Congress Cataloging-in-Publication Data

Names: Esposito, Cameron, author.
Title: Save yourself / Cameron Esposito.
Description: First edition. | New York : Grand Central Publishing, 2020.
Identifiers: LCCN 2019026134 (print) | LCCN 2019026135 (ebook) | ISBN 9781455591435 (hardcover) | ISBN 9781455591442 (ebook)
Subjects: LCSH: Esposito, Cameron. | Women comedians—United States—Biography. | Lesbians—United States—Biography.
Classification: LCC PN2287.E754 A3 2020 (print) | LCC PN2287.E754 (ebook) | DDC 792.7/6028092 [B]—dc23
LC record available at https://lccn.loc.gov/2019026134
LC ebook record available at https://lccn.loc.gov/2019026135

ISBNs: 978-1-4555-9143-5 (hardcover), 978-1-4555-9144-2 (ebook)

Printed in the United States of America

LSC-C

10 9 8 7 6 5 4 3 2 1

to every queer kid,
be you little and bitty or all grown-up

INTRODUCTION

Growing up in the 1980s and '90s in suburban Chicago, I didn't know gay people were real. I thought gay people and leprechauns were mythical creatures for parades with hats and buckles, and some of that's true.

I do own several buckles.

Before *The L Word* was pitched, when Lena Waithe and Kate McKinnon were kids, lesbians existed but I couldn't see 'em. Or hear 'em. Or look 'em up because THERE WAS NO INTERNET.

Ellen had a scripted show on the air and I wasn't allowed to watch it.

Mx. DeGeneres hadn't yet voiced a fish, created a talk show suitable for any doctor's office, or even publicly come out, but my very Catholic parents sensed the cut of her Birkenstock and your grandpa Cameron wasn't allowed to watch her show.

At twenty, when I realized I was gay, I imagined I'd spend my adulthood alone, a friendless lesbian match girl at society's window pleading to be let in, and my eternity in hell, barbecuing alongside monsters who killed people or ate people or ate people they killed.

Then I fell in love, found comedy, and met some people who weren't Catholic, or weren't as Catholic as me. Slowly, over years, I worked to accept myself as perfectly fucking normal and okay.

Now, because of my job, I often present only that part of me to the world. But there are other parts.

There's this scene in the 1972 film version of *Cabaret* where Liza Minnelli's character, Sally Bowles, is backstage, about to walk out and perform at the Kit Kat Klub. It's 1931. It's Berlin. And things are about to be awful. Also, Sally's just had an abortion, which is messing with her bod, and she's emotionally raw because she's kinda going through two breakups at once, and THEN THERE'S THE FUCKING NAZIS TO THINK ABOUT. Anyway, *Cabaret* is a very good movie.

The scene I'm talking about is maybe two seconds long. I first watched it with my Big Deal Ex*—you know, the one who was my first real adult I'm-in-my-midtwenties partner who I thought I'd maybe marry even though same-sex marriage was then illegal? My Big Deal Ex was a modern dancer, obviously, like my older sister, and showed me *Cabaret* because the dang movie is directed by Bob Fosse and when you spend a lot of time around dancers you learn that apparently it is possible to "tuck your tailbone" and that I should, in fact, "tuck my tailbone," and you also learn about Fosse and Tharp and Ailey and Baryshnikov (before Carrie Bradshaw).

Here's the scene:

It starts out dark. The curtains are closed. Sally is alone, head down, looking nowhere at nothing, and it's just her vulnerable, real, suffering self. Then the curtains open, light floods over her, and in the time it takes her to raise her head, her face—her whole being—is transformed: With a wide red grin and confident shoulders she walks out onstage. And when she does, she stops time. She owns herself and you and you've agreed to be owned and you're happy about it.

And that's what it feels like every time I do stand-up. Each time I step onstage, I leave my small, worried self behind and become a version of me that is power and projection. Onstage I'm your daddy. Backstage I'm upset and critical. So maybe your father?

Here's just one example: It's September 3, 2013. I'm performing on *The Late Late Show with Craig Ferguson*. It's my first time on network television. The curtain opens and I walk out onstage and, honestly, crush, Sally-style. Craig and Jay Leno, the other guest that night, interrupt my set and call me over to the couch (the biggest compliment a stand-up comic can get) and I sit between them, my feet not touching the ground even though I'm sitting in a fairly low chair because I'm the size of a Tamagotchi. My then-partner is in the greenroom, watching the taping beside the show's producers, and the room erupts with cheers when I'm invited to the couch. My parents watch the broadcast and I give 'em a shout-out. It's one year to the day since I moved to Los Angeles, and my hope is that this TV appearance will put them at ease. That they'll scream, "She made it!" at one another before collapsing into each other's arms, exhausted.

Because there was a long time when they—and I—thought I wouldn't make it. Not as a comic, but as a human. As a queer gay lesbian human being, which I am.

People frequently come up to me after shows and tell me I am the first out gay person they've met. This still happens. Today, the day you are reading this, this happened. I'm sure of it. Some are straight and I've "changed their mind about queer folks." Some are queer folks raised with a few more queer characters on TV but still isolated in the real world, who see, in me, an example of a possible future they might have, with a career and an extensive collection of button-downs. I'm proud of that, but it feels a little like only watching that one scene in *Cabaret*, and I'd like to tell the whole fucking queer-as-hell story.

This is a book about the small, worried guy left backstage.

It isn't a sidebar to a straight person's rebirth—I don't give a makeover or plan a wedding or get a couple back together. It's not a tragedy. I don't die at the end of this book, having finally decided to kiss the girl. It's honest and bumpy and scared and sexy and real.

It's the dyke's tale my younger self needed to read.

And I hope you enjoy it.

―∿―

*Cammy's Note: It would seem that as this book publishes, I will have an even Bigger Deal Ex. It's an excruciatingly painful loss that I chose not to write about in this book except here where I'll say: GODDAMNIT.

LITTLE GAY KID

Today, I am a Big Gay Adult, but I got my start as a Little Gay Kid (LGK).

In between, I was several other things, including a preteen battling her body, the proudly abstinent girlfriend of the captain of the football team, and an actual Republican. So it was a bit of a winding path from Little Gay Kid to Big Gay Adult.

I grew up the tough, square-jawed middle sister in a fiercely Italian, very Catholic family. My hometown is an idyllic suburb fifteen miles west of Chicago called Western Springs, and can best be described as quaint—it's like the village in *Hot Fuzz*, but no one's gone missing and instead, all thirteen thousand inhabitants are happy and fulfilled. Across from our George Carlin–less *Shining Time Station*, there's a fruit store called—wait for it— Fruit Store. The two-block strip of downtown holds a butcher, a baker, and several places wherein candlesticks can be purchased, though not from their original maker. The baker makes legendary smiley-face cookies frosted with either pink or yellow buttercream. EVEN THE COOKIES ARE HAPPY.

We also had a literal milkman a good forty years after the rest of the country decided to suck it up and go to the store to get their own damn milk. Not us! We lived blissfully behind the times in a land where front yards were large, divorce rates were low, nearly everyone was white, and all those white people went to church on Sunday.

And goddamn if it wasn't friendly there. We knew our neighbor's neighbor's dogs' names. Every June, we'd put costumes on those dogs and on ourselves and march in the annual Pet Parade held one town over. There was AYSO soccer in the summer, king-size candy bar trick-or-treating in the fall, caroling in the winter, and Rollerblading in the spring.

Now, when I say I was raised very Catholic, I mean I attended Catholic school, said rosaries during my free time, and eventually became an altar server (a sort of priest's assistant and rather new role in the Church for gals because, in Catholicism, women are for listening). I had this tiny plastic bottle marked HOLY WATER that contained—you guessed it—holy water, which is water a priest has been nearby and said some words over, and I used it to bless myself before falling asleep under this huge poster of a pretty scared-looking polar bear wandering through the snow that I had framed because, myself a scared white animal wandering through a white world, it just felt so me.

My family prayed before dinner and had Filet-o-Fish on Fridays during Lent. My parents both grew up in the kind of Italian Catholic families that made their own wine in the basement and their own sausage in the kitchen. They attended Catholic grade school and Catholic high school and met at a Catholic college. When it came time to raise their own family, they started us early with all Catholicism, all the time. My mom and I said Hail Marys together as she braided my hair. My dad, a lawyer, often stopped at a chapel downtown to pray before going to court, which would be unfair to opposing counsel if prayer affected legal outcomes.

My sister Allyson and I played church-inspired games. One favorite was Mass, in which we would line up our stuffed animals or our grandparents, whichever was around, for a quick sermon about *Muppet Babies*. My sister and I took turns priesting and my nana took the Eucharist with a solemn "Body of Christ" and an "Amen." If those years of at-home games of Mass taught me anything, it would be to recommend thinly sliced bananas or Better Cheddars as a great stand-in for Eucharist (and if you use bananas, may I recommend leaving them out for a bit after slicing to allow the fruit to brown up a bit and more naturally match the skin tone of real Jesus, who, I was shocked to learn in college, was Middle Eastern and so probably looked Middle Eastern).

Another beloved game was Birth of Christ: Allyson was Mary and I was Joseph (naturally), and she would deliver a Cabbage Patch Kids doll into a brown piece of Tupperware with a yellow pom-pom inside—the "hay" was essential to make the manger feel true to life. The most complicated game was Jesus/Moses. During the winter, we'd walk on the frozen ice crusts between driveways. If you made it all the way from one driveway to the next without falling through to the layer of soft snow underneath: Jesus. But if you fell through: Moses. (Which is a gross misunderstanding of Moses's relationship to water, but Catholics don't really read the Bible. We're more of a "What Does the Pope Say the Bible Says?" kinda crew.)

And if you thought all of this was chill, my parents also sort of raised my sisters and me like marines. Their number one rule of Espositohood: Don't Leave Your Sisters Behind. An intense family motto, really. To this day I'm not totally sure what they were preparing us for, because we straight-up lived in the suburbs and that sounds like something from *Band of Brothers*. The house I grew up in was very warm and full of love—my parents often slow-danced in our kitchen—but it was strict and stressful, too. I was never supposed to operate outside the family's collective will, and I was expected to Spider-Man my privilege ("with great power comes great responsibility") and make sure my sisters and all future generations of our line were pulled up to the next rung on the ladder. That's a lot to carry. I have a fucked-up right shoulder from metaphorically pulling that weight and, yes, metaphors can hurt your shoulder.

Allyson is three years older than I, but we were raised like twins, although I once said as much to Tegan Quin (of the twin band Tegan and Sara) and she looked at me like I was out of my mind. Oh well! Sorry, actual twins. What I mean is that we acted as counterpoints to one another. (Is that twins? Whatever.) My little sister, Britton, wasn't born until Allyson was ten and I was seven. Britton was The Baby and The Witch (she was born on Halloween and has one of those personalities where she can speak to the moon) and Allyson and I were the First Two—best buds, but also polar opposites with none of the same interests or hobbies.

Allyson was a careful, delicate kid who studied ballet and talked softly. She choreographed dances and alphabetized her toys while I jumped off the tops of swing sets and yelled a lot. She collected Barbies. I collected Kens. I had six of them. Mattel didn't actually make six varieties of Ken at the time, by the way. I had multiples of the same model that I differentiated based on "moles" created by errant paint drips. I'd pop a Ken into his best sleeveless snap-on tuxedo onesie and send him out for a date with Barbie—or, scandalously, with Skipper, Barbie's sister and closest friend. All the Kens shared a ride—a hot pink T-top—and they looked glorious in it. I couldn't wait to grow into a tuxedo of my own.

It was like Allyson and I lived in a binary system, where she was the daughter of the family and I was the son. Since both these slots were filled by the time she was born, Britton the Witch kind of did her own thing, including, for a solid year of her young life, identifying as a dog. She wore a Dalmatian costume every day and would only eat on the floor. We were just another family in Pleasantville with a girl daughter, a girl son, a human-shaped dog, and a milkman.

As the girl son, I was and continue to be protective of both my sisters, even though Allyson is older. I was very invested in savior behavior, which felt very male to me, based on movies, TV, and that dude Jesus. Allyson was demure and if the word "femme" means anything, she was that. If anyone messed with her I'd throw my much younger and smaller body in front of hers, yelling, "LEAVE MY SISTER ALONE!" When she started to date and her boyfriend was a dick, I logged on to my parents' AOL account and emailed him, *Don't ever talk to my sister again! By the way, I'm 12!*

In case you think the difference in our gendering made me the only tough guy in the Esposito family, Allyson has a completely solid roundhouse kick and Britton will lure you in with her yogic exterior only to FUCK YOU UP. Which is to say, I have physically fought both my sisters many times. We played with dolls, but we also sat on each other's heads and farted. Our sisterhood was boundaryless, full of screaming, tackling, and squeezing. And A LOT of cuddling, too. We were so in love with each other—we still are—and our childhood was one big montage of the three of us repeatedly flinging our entire bodies at each other. We each had our own room, but on weekends and holidays we'd always sleep together in one of our twin beds.

Sometimes Allyson would try to pretend to be older and cooler than all that. "Get out of here, lesbians!" she'd scream when Britton and I piled into her bed. Yes, she frequently called us lesbians. No, lesbians don't sleep with their actual sisters. But when Allyson slung that then-contextless word around our house, Britton would be like, "I will kiss you on your LIPS!" and then do it. My dad kisses his male friends on the lips as a greeting to this day, so this was all very normal in my extremely Italian household.

God, I love my sisters. They feel like parts of my own body sometimes.

Tangentially related to gender, I spent my childhood constantly injured. Some of the injuries had to do with my reckless swing-set-jumping attitude—like when I broke my arm in three places bailing off a bike at full speed—but many happened because I've never been able to see a goddamned thing.

I mean, I can see, but you better be three inches from my face, because I am awfully nearsighted and always have been. Being a little kid with glasses, that's one thing. You'll smash your glasses playing basketball or lose them in the ocean. You might get called Four Eyes or some other nonsense. If you were a glasses kid, I feel you. It's tough walking in the rain in those things, and it's super creepy going to bed when you can't quite figure out what that blob in the corner might be (it's always just a pile of clothes). But let me lay this on you: I also had crossed eyes and wore an eye patch for eight years of my childhood.

One morning when I was two I woke up and walked downstairs to greet my mom (this is a story I've been told; I do not remember anything before I was five except for one moment I'm gonna mention in the next paragraph—GET EXCITED FOR THAT!) and my right eye had lost its iris. My left eye still contained the brown iris I'd gone to sleep with and my right eye was totally white, a blank eyeball. So this appropriately SCARED THE SHIT out of my mom, who called my dad and had him paged on the golf course (yes, I had a privileged golfing-parent childhood) with something like "No emergency but if Mr. Esposito could please come to the clubhouse, that'd be great. Your wife just called and your girl son's eyeball is blank." From what I'm told, when my dad got home I was blissfully running in circles in the front yard, likely because my newly unbalanced one-eyed vision had me thinking that was a straight line and I haven't been straight since.

No, but for real, I was definitely gay before that. I remember being in my mom's womb and being like "I'm a Shane," and it wasn't until almost twenty years later when *The L Word* debuted that I learned what that meant. And of course that is a joke and not the thing I remember from before I was five because that's actually in the next paragraph. This paragraph is simply an aside. I am a Shane, though, not an Alice. Don't you tell me I'm an Alice!

Anyway, my parents rushed me to the hospital, where the doctors reassured them by saying, "Is this a girl? We can't tell from the bowl cut. Okay, well, she didn't lose her iris, it's just off to the side, facing back into her skull, and we think it's a brain tumor because that's what makes eyes cross this drastically and quickly. Oh wait, never mind, we did many tests and her brain is A-okay. Whoopsie-daisy. It's just that one of her eyes has super weak muscles on the side. And sorry, just to be double clear: Is this a girl?" So after those two things happened, I was scheduled for laser eye muscle surgery (*pew-pew*) and I got a crapload of presents because I survived a brain tumor I didn't have. I remember the giraffe nightgown I wore to the hospital the day of the surgery—THERE'S THE MEMORY—most likely because, even at that time, I'm sure I was like, "Ugh. A dress? Y'all couldn't get a Ken tux together for the occasion? I MIGHT DIE ON THE TABLE IN A FREAKING DRESS."

I had that first surgery very quickly, because there's a chance with crossed eyes that your brain will get mad about seeing images that don't combine well and choose to blind you in one eye to save you the trouble of double vision. Yeah, the crossing creates double vision, making it really hard to not hit your head on *everything*. After surgery, I had to wear tiny adorable humiliating children's glasses that looked almost exactly like the ones Dustin Hoffman wears in *Tootsie*, a movie about how hard it is to be a man in the entertainment industry because all the good roles go to older women.

And not just glasses. Also an eye patch. Here's the drill: I patched my strong eye (left) so my weak eye (right) had to actually buck up and get some seeing done. Without the patch I'd let my left eye do the looking, oftentimes turning my head to the right so that my left eye could fully take over while I rocked myself slowly and rhythmically in a cross-legged position, seated directly in front of the television because I also couldn't see distance, though we didn't know that yet. I guess my parents could have been like,

"Um, sweetie, this tilted-head rocking-too-close-to-the-TV thing is terrifying and we're curious if you are yourself a ghost or have been visited by ghosts," but instead they just yelled, "BOTH EYES," meaning I was supposed to straighten out my face during the times when the patch was off.

Which really wasn't that often. As a kid, that patch was my life. And I'm not talking about a black pirate eye patch. I had to wear a disposable Band-Aid material eye patch. The patch was the same color as my flesh and, from a distance, made it seem as if I was perpetually winking, or doing a long-term impression of Sloth from *The Goonies*.

The company that made these patches must have felt bad for the kids who had to wear them. To soften the blow of having to wear a flesh flap, they put a few stickers in with the patches. "Use 'em to decorate," they said, woefully unaware that an eye patch can't be cool. Plus, the specific stickers added insult to injury. Each was perfectly round, the size of a penny, and featured a bucolic farm scene printed in only navy blue, tan, and brown. I guess little eye-patched kids were meant to show up at school and say, "Oh, you've got a Lisa Frank iridescent pony on your Trapper Keeper? Well, I've got a drab vignette of a deer, a silo, and an owl on my eye patch!" Luckily, I was also chubby, had a bowl cut, *and* insisted upon only wearing red jeans, so the eye patch blended nicely with the overall tragedy of my childhood aesthetic. I think my patch had a great influence on my later career in comedy. When you're a little gay Sloth pirate running around the suburbs, you better be hilarious. And I am.

When I first came out to my parents, they insisted that there had been no signs that I was gay in my childhood. There were, in fact, seven billion. Maybe we were looking for different signs. Perhaps they had expected to walk in on me kissing an entire softball team whilst wearing a vest made of Subarus, or as a baby to have cried until they put Melissa Etheridge's and k.d. lang's albums on at the same time, which can't be done without ripping the space-time continuum. Those voices are too strong, and if united must be fought from within the confines of a giant robot driven by Idris Elba.

By the way, Little Gay Kids are the best, except of course if our hands turn everything to ice and then we have to wear gloves and can't build snowmen with our siblings. The entertainment industry has been copping our steeze and bestowing it upon the coolest characters for quite a while. And why wouldn't they? We are the ones who push things forward. We're creative, we're innovative, and if LGK Idgie Threadgoode's appearance in the movie *Fried Green Tomatoes* taught us anything, we're pretty much the reason women can wear pants.

Why are Little Gay Kids so creative? Probably because we are working hard to make sense of our own identities. We know there is something different about us but can't figure out what it might be. We often don't have the language or space to ponder our sexualities or gender presentations. So we feel like outsiders or bystanders or both.

Perhaps the best way I can start to identify the hallmarks of my LGK childhood would be to present some of the greatest hits from my Little Gay Kid-oweens. I grew up loving October 31, and not just for the monster mash or the graveyard smash. When you're an LGK, Halloween is THE BEST. It's the only day when you can dress exactly as you feel comfy with no backlash. I mean, probably with A LITTLE backlash, but way less than usual.

CAMERON ESPOSITO'S LITTLE GAY KID-OWEENS: A GREATEST HITS COMPILATION

AGE 8: BLOODY PIRATE

My birthday falls close to Halloween, and I had some girls over for a dress-up birthday party when I turned eight. The other girls were things like Jem or a kitten or a nurse. I went as a pirate and kept leaving my own party to add sweet effects to my costume—once to draw on a beard that went all the way up to my eye sockets, and once to dip my best plastic bowie knife in red paint to simulate the blood of my enemies. I think some of the girls were unnerved by my upgrades, but I didn't give ONE FUCK because the added toughness put me in the exact right frame of mind to kill the shit out of my piñata. Candy from heaven, muthafuckahs!

Grade: B-

Age 10: Robin Hood

I was really into whittling my own bows and arrows at this point in my childhood. Mostly, I'd use them to shoot into the yard of my parents' long-suffering back-door neighbors. This was after I had both snapped the heads off all their flowers because I thought they were "haunted" and dug up a power line in their garden because I thought they had buried a body there. What can I say? I was a spooked-out kid. And they were old and I had seen the Tom Hanks film *The 'Burbs* and there was a white-haired dude in that movie who MURDERED PEOPLE. Anyway, this costume was great. Green tights, and one of my mom's chunky belts over a green tunic that maybe I constructed from a pillow case or something? I tied it all together with a homemade felt quiver that kept spinning upside down and dumping out all my arrows— that was the WORST!   *Grade: B+*

Age 11: Charlie Chaplin

I spent my early childhood donning culturally acceptable gal garb like colorful Multiples-brand clothing separates—cotton tubes of neon fabric that could be worn as a tube top or tube bottom. Nothing could be more confusing to an LGK than a skirt that could also be a shirt. I'd ask myself, if this fabric tube could be both, then wasn't it also neither? By the time I was eleven, I was hankering to spend some time in menswear. A Halloween spent as Charlie Chaplin was the perfect excuse to wear a full suit and pay homage to some rad Hollywood shit. Did you say full suit? I did! What about a mustache? You bet! Unfortunately, they don't make child-size novelty canes, so my Chaplin cane was twice my height and I ended up looking like a suited wizard or shepherd Hitler. *Grade:* A-

AGE 12: GARFIELD

By this time, I was deep into Becoming a Woman™, and thanks to my down-the-street neighbor Chloe, this Halloween I finally had the tools to flaunt it. Chloe's mom mentioned to mine that Chloe had a Garfield costume from maybe the previous year or perhaps from a visit to hell, where Chloe met with Satan and he provided her with the Hottest Costume in Terms of Temperature Not Sexiness Which Is Fine I Was a Child but Too Warm. Let me describe this Garfield outfit: dirty-melted-orange-sherbet-colored plush enrobed my pubescent body from toe to tip including shoe covers and giant smiling head with a full cat face and my human face peeking out the mouth. My friends were a '60s poodle-skirt-wearing sock-hopper and Judy Jetson and we walked the neighborhood while I sweated my furry suit an even darker shade of orange and cut weight for the upcoming wrestling championship I did not have. *Grade:* A+

In my Halloween-costume heyday, before I turned thirteen and realized only *kids* go trick-or-treating and I was *definitely* not a kid, it seemed like the outside world was mostly fine with me exercising my right to butch it up. I was grubby and brutish, and, seeing two of everything when I jumped off a slide or popped a wheelie on the curb, just as likely to land on my face as my feet, which meant I was scabby, a walking bruise, perpetually draped in some sports equipment or other. So yes, I was often mistaken for a boy, by doctors about to laser my eye into place or by anyone else.

There was something about other girls that seemed to prevent this mistake from happening to them, and it wasn't because they looked all that much girlier. Certainly in our elementary school years none of us had boobs yet, and I wasn't the only girl in my class with short hair. It was something beyond what I could identify as a preteen attending Catholic school in a pre–Samira Wiley world—a fundamental difference that surfaced again and again.

For instance, when I was in fourth grade, I auditioned for the part of Christopher Columbus in the school play, *In Quest of Columbus*. I didn't yet know that Christopher Columbus was a non-holiday-deserving smallpox fairy or what playing him entailed—which by the way was a total of four lines—but he was the titular character and, I assumed, star of the show, so unbeknownst to my parents and without encouragement from any of my teachers, I went out for the part. I figured all the other gals in my class were being shy by not auditioning. It never once crossed my mind that they wouldn't want to dress in drag and sing in an affected baritone. For the record, I landed the part, but only after my teachers called home to get my parents' permission. It was a minor scandal that my folks said yes, which I love them for, though I think perhaps my grade school's scandal scale is off, since not one complaint was lodged the year the drama teacher taped peyos to the sides of the kids' faces who starred in *Fiddler on the Roof JR*.

Perhaps by now you are beginning to catch on that I've always been masculine of center, gender nonconforming, or whatever better words might have come down the pipeline by the time you're reading this. Cameron is a genderless name, and especially during my bowl cut era, strangers often called me "young man" or referred to me as my sisters' brother. In my early childhood, I had no problem expressing masculinity. During family trips to Florida, I begged my parents to let me play on the beach in just bikini bottoms, with the warm sun on my bare chest.

But soon "not girly enough" became "bad." I started wearing girls' bathing suits and would still be mistaken for a boy. This felt shameful—to be trying to "fit" as a girl and unable to do so.

You know how some people, like off the top of my head Superman or Batman or Spider-Man or Buffy the Vampire Slayer, lead double lives? Somewhere around the same time that my internal shame alarm started going off, I started leading one, too. I joked instead of crying. I shoved my pain way down deep inside and put a joke on top, getting funnier and funnier by the minute.

I didn't have the language to say, "It seems you're noticing that my gender presents differently from what you're used to. That's partly because it's the mid-'80s and we don't have a ton of opportunities to see many different types of people, especially in an upper-middle-class white suburban neighborhood like ours. Boy, will the internet blow all of our minds a decade from now! Anyway, many of us gender-nonconforming folks exist in the world, have for centuries, and it's actually totally fine—in fact, it's great! There's nothing wrong with me or you, and coming to understand my own gender expression will be one of the most freeing experiences I'll have in my next two decades on this planet. I wish the same to you!"

I did have the language to clown around, and I'm grateful for that. It's how I survived. Today, though, I'm working to build my emotional language, too. Vulnerability makes me extremely uncomfortable, but I've lived without vulnerability and that's lonely as hell. I still carry shame over not being the woman culture expects me to be. Just last week, I got called a dyke while walking down my own street by one of my neighbors—and not as a friendly greeting between dykes. My reaction, after wanting to punch the dude in the nose, was to feel bad about myself. So I'm the one that's embarrassed? Even though he's a jerk, and I know where he lives? But yes, I was embarrassed about my Hawaiian shirt and jean jacket. How am I ever supposed to heal or feel safe?

Well, for one, by telling someone about it. On that particular day I called a friend and told that story and cried a little. And then I met a friend for coffee and told the story and frowned a little. Then I put a small amount of my dog's poop in the driveway of the person who called me a dyke, just for safekeeping. Then, only then, did I write a joke about it. I shared it as a person first and a comic second.

I have that photo of myself dressed as Garfield for Halloween on my fridge. I look at it every day. I love that LGK. If I met her today, my heart would swell for her. What a brave, nonconforming sweetheart. What a bulky outfit. The world may not love her, or some folks in the world may not, but I do. I love you, little Cammy. Never change.

HAVING A BODY

A few years ago, I filmed a sketch for *Comedy Bang! Bang!* on IFC. I played a server and, in a replay of my *In Quest of Columbus* days, had four lines, and I don't know if I fucked them up or not because I don't watch myself on TV. There's one thing I know I didn't fuck up, though: standing in only my bra in front of a stranger and being all chill about it.

I didn't know until I arrived on set that I was supposed to provide my own wardrobe options. That's not a weird request for a four-line role on a sketch-type show, just a message that somehow hadn't been passed along to me. I didn't know I was supposed to bring "a variety of white button-down shirts," and no one from the cast of *Party Down* was on set to give me theirs, so I ended up filming in the black jeans and navy blue T-shirt I wore every day at the time.

I'm not kidding about it being the same T-shirt and jeans. Well, not the *same* same shirt and jeans. I owned six pairs of the same black jeans and twenty of the same navy blue T-shirts. When not onstage, that's what I wore every day. Andrew Dice Clay had all black everything. Andrew W.K.'s got all white. Black jeans/navy tee was my look. I was Andrew Dice Gay of Andrew W.Gays. This was before Elizabeth Holmes was the subject of one thousand TV shows. The same-outfit solution meant only "I'm a genius."

Well, not the *same* outfit. Sometimes, to keep things caliente, I'd add a jean jacket. I was so committed to this outfit that I gave myself heatstroke refusing to replace the jeans with shorts when performing in 104-degree heat at Bonnaroo one year. I chose to barf *on* the medical tent instead of wearing shorts onstage. Like, I was standing outside the med tent, having been rushed there in a golf cart with a siren on top, when an EMT asked, "What seems to be the problem?" and I Jackson Pollocked all over the side of the tent. Not a smart choice by any stretch of the imagination, but the woman who treated me for heatstroke did have a rattail she'd been growing for twenty-five years (I asked), so even idiotic choices can lead to beautiful memories. By the way, I want to add that I have evolved far beyond this and now mix it up all the time by exclusively wearing button-down shirts and motorcycle jackets.

I was wearing this standard ensemble when I showed up on set. Seeing me all T-shirted out, the wardrobe department hustled to try to get a few top options—toptions—together for me to wear. I vetoed a sleeveless number with zippers due to my end-stage farmer's tan (my forearms declare my Italian heritage with a bronzed "Esposito!" but my shoulders are pale as Dita Von Teese riding a tauntaun on Hoth). Also, zippers DO NOT belong on tops, a lesson I learned in hindsight only, looking back at mid-'90s photos of myself wearing floral neon polyester zip-up polos from Contempo Casuals.

When a low-cut, backless cardigan was suggested next, I decided to humor them and pop it on as a gesture of "See, I'm not completely difficult!" Besides, when would I next have the opportunity to wear a low-cut, backless cardigan, since I am always buying shirts that have a back *or* a front, if not a back *and* a front?

(If you need help imagining a low-cut, backless cardigan, picture a scarf with buttons. Even the fact that it exists is a miracle!) We went through a dozen more numbers better suited to a Daisy Buchanan type (she's just out of reach!) than to my particular gender (fighter pilot) before it was decided that the black jeans/ navy tee I arrived in was a capital choice of outfits and would be perfect for my role of "Server."

Here's the thing about wardrobe: you change right in front of them. To get my black jeans/navy tee approved, I'd stood shirtless in front of two gals for about a half hour. Now, they are pros and they see it all the time and my body ain't that special. It's like at Victoria's Secret, when, if you will allow the bra measurers into the fitting room, they'll just zoom their hands around your under-wire and pinch a cup or two before you can blink. It's their job; nudity or bra-dity just isn't a big deal to them. But it is a big deal to me.

The first time someone called me fat in front of a big group of people I was at a family farm in Middle of Nowhere, Wisconsin (or possibly Indiana), for a barbecue. You know that period of time when kids just sort of stretch—when we go from compact energy bombs into exhausted stalks of mostly leg? I didn't have that moment. I've always looked the same way I do now, which is generally low to the ground and solid, like what I imagine a spark plug resembles, except the only thing I know about cars is that they can fly between buildings but only in Dubai when driven by Vin Diesel.

The family farm was owned by the grandparents of one of my classmates, and every summer, a big group of kids and their parents were invited to spend the day there. It was absurdly adorable, complete with a white clapboard farmhouse and an actual swimming hole. It was the kind of sweet little place that'd harbor mutants behind a small door under the stairs so as to better murder you after sunset. Our parents would chat over beers while us kids mucked about in the water, getting out only when another kid dared us to touch the electric fence that kept the neighbors' cows penned in.

The summer I was nine, we had been swimming for a bit when the electric fence dares started up. I couldn't wait until my turn. I'd touched the fence the year before and basically coasted on that reputation ever since. This year I planned to do it without stopping for a towel first, sprinting over to the fence still dripping in a move I'd call "hairdryer in the bathtub." I imagined myself back at school the following September, walking the halls with a Danny Zuko leather jacket over my school uniform. "How was my summer? I'll tell you! I TOUCHED A DAMN ELECTRIC FENCE. WHILE I WAS WET. Oh, and I'm nine. Hey, can you pass me those cigarettes? I'm gonna hold 'em but not smoke 'em because I don't smoke." Then I'd open my locker by punching it and make my way to class.

Some kids took a pass. *Jurassic Park* wouldn't come out for another couple of years, but it was as if we predicted its best scene. "You hold on too long and your hair will scorch up. Good news is, you may get to meet Laura Dern." Finally, the dares came around to me. "Cameron," someone said, "I dare you to touch that fence," pointing across the swimming hole to the closest section.

"Uh, YEAH I'll touch it," I answered. "I won't even dry off first." A hush went out across the swimming hole as I made my way to the dock to pull myself out. My friends swam along with me, making a semicircle near the dock to get a better view.

As anyone who grew up on *The Little Mermaid* will tell you, the wet hair flip is the most powerful of all the water moves. And the weakest water move is sex because the water washes away all lubrication so please stop putting that in your teen-focused TV shows and films. Anyway. Hair flip. Mermaid. Winds. Words.

That's what I imagined I looked like as I got to the dock, dipped my face into the water one more time, and yanked my head back with all my might. My bowl cut tore through the air—majestic— and I gave my best Ariel-on-a-rock-with-waves-crashing push-up out of the swimming hole and showed off my swim team Speedo, an article of clothing I loved and felt comfortable in because it was a girl's suit that didn't make me feel all weird and sexy or put my not-yet-boobs on display.

I'd started taking swim classes at age two, and by nine, I was a Michael Phelps (after a few joints)–level swimmer with swim team practice every morning during the summer. My specialty? Breaststroke, of course. That's the one that looks like how a frog swims, and is named after an activity I'd excel at later in life, too. Sidebar: A pool is also a great place to hang if you're a klutzy cross-eyed kid. It is nigh impossible to fall within water.

At the end of the dock stood someone's younger cousin, a first grader, holding a handful of soggy Cheetos. He took one look at me, dripping wet and on the precipice of triumph, and said, in a voice loud enough to be heard by friends and cows alike, two words that completely deflated me. Two words I had said to myself before and still hear in my head almost every day.

"You're fat."

I wish I'd slapped the Cheetos out of that kid's hand. Instead, I went directly into the farmhouse to find a bathroom and cry (which was terrible, although it also forestalled my impending electrocution), because as soon as those two words were out in the air, I knew I'd been dreading the moment when someone would finally say them aloud.

Now, like I said, this was the first time I was called fat in front of a large group of people. It was not the first time my body was openly discussed. A few years ago I had an old Christmas video converted from VHS to DVD so I could play it at a live show. The last time I'd watched the video I was in high school and I vaguely remembered that it had some funny moments. I knew Allyson, then ten, gave a four-and-a-half-minute explanation of the board game Girl Talk that was Adult Swim–caliber batshit amazing, and I knew I went nuts after receiving a black Ken, the only present I specifically asked for that year. I had taken to including my Winston the Ghostbuster action figure to add some diversity to my crew of three white Kens, but you couldn't change Winston's clothes.

Anyway, the video starts with Allyson killing it describing the Girl Talk zit stickers, cuts to me screaming, "FINALLY!" at the top of my lungs as I hold up an Afro-ed Ken. Then the video gets sad. I'm still in the center of the frame, slow-dancing with my Ken. From off-camera, Allyson says, "The best part of Girl Talk are the questions. They ask things like what would you change about yourself?"

My dad chimes in, also off-camera, "And what would you change, Allyson?"

"I think...nothing?" she says.

"Well, if you had to pick one thing?" my dad pushes.

"I guess maybe I wouldn't have glasses?"

Then my dad addresses me. "And what about you, Cameron? What would you change?" I turn to the camera and wordlessly pat my tummy. "Yeah," my dad says. "I'd get rid of my belly, too."

I was seven.

In my family, that interaction wasn't odd. I grew up with Italian grandmothers on both sides feeding me treats to fatten me up. My mom's family is from the part of Ohio that operates as Appalachia, where Southern accents and cowboy boots abound. Just across the Ohio River from West Virginia, my mom's hometown of Gallipolis and many of the surrounding towns once relied heavily on river commerce as their main industry. When that demand died down, so did Second Avenue, the town's main thoroughfare. A Walmart moved in nearby and the town began to look like a lot of America. Empty storefronts. Full Walmart parking lot.

Gallipolis is also the hometown of Bob Evans, from the roadside breakfast chain restaurant. One time in my youth, my dad almost hit that guy with our family station wagon. "It's Bob Evans!" he yelled, slamming on the brakes and leaving us all pretty hungry for biscuits. And *The Mothman Prophecies*? That Richard Gere movie about a, um, mothman who's a moth and a man who comes to warn townspeople about a bridge collapse? That's based on a real thing that happened in my mom's hometown while she was in high school. People said they saw a mothman. And then a bridge collapsed. Prior to his death, my grandfather, a man who once said he was unarmed because he was only carrying his "boot gun," insisted that the mothman was actually his friend Earl, who was a peeping tom and "an odd duck." (Sidenote: Why was he friends with a peeping tom?)

We drove the ten hours from Western Springs and stayed for a few weeks in Gallipolis every summer when I was a kid. My sisters and I slept in a spare bedroom that was lined with (locked) gun cabinets. My grandfather hunted to provide food for the family, and my mom had grown up eating wild game like rabbit, deer, squirrel, and lots of organ meat, which she hated. As a result, we pretty much only ate baked skinless chicken breast in our household. No one in Gallipolis went to the gym or ate steamed veggies. Salads were whatever could be encased in Jell-O. Dentistry was cost prohibitive and many of my family members were missing teeth. My grandfather was often out of work and my grandmother's business was a hair and tanning salon run out of a trailer in her backyard that my dad almost burned down one time with a firework.

Thank god I grew up going to Gallipolis. My mom had worked at McDonald's to put herself through college and my dad had shoveled asphalt to put himself through law school. On both sides, my family was very recently middle class, but my experience of growing up in Western Springs included proximity to extreme wealth. The town next to us was posh and fucking rich. Houses there had elevators, fountains, pools, landscaping, horses, and landscaping horses (horses who do landscaping). If I'd only seen my town and the town next door, I might have turned out like, "Oh, my family is broke. We use the pool at the country club like paupers."

But I digress. What I'm trying to say is that my mom's side of the family ate like Southerners *and* like Italians. Whatever food wasn't pasta was certainly fried and/or had been shot by my grandpa in the backyard. For my grandmother specifically, this led to a slew of health problems. She had a stroke, a heart attack, type 2 diabetes, and then she battled cancer. Of course, this wasn't all diet—some folks eat heavy saturated fats and live to smoke a pack on their hundred and first birthday. Those people are French.

My mom's mother's name was Eva. She was tough—the kind of human lovingly described by family as "ornery"—and her thick country accent and array of needles for insulin injections scared the hell out of me. Her stroke had paralyzed one of her arms, something that also frightened me as a child. I never asked her any questions about what it was like losing the use of her arm and I never heard anyone commend her for continuing her career as a hairdresser with one working hand. She was a survivor; I wish I had actually known her.

She died at seventy, reaching for the phone. She had a massive heart attack and must have been trying to call for help. My grandpa Bob, a man who seemed to hold all jobs and no job the entire time I knew him, was out glad-handing neighbors or buying Lotto scratchers or folding gum wrappers into tiny swans on a bench outside the local buffet, and she likely passed wondering what the heck he was out doing anyway, which, from my vantage point of their marriage, had been sort of how she lived. Eva hadn't been particularly overweight, but after a long battle with one health crisis after another, her doctors advised that changing her diet—adding in lower-fat foods and more raw fruits and veggies—could prolong her life. She didn't change it. And she died alone and hoping for help, which scared the shit out of my mom.

My family had already begun to adopt some of the advice my grandmother had been given. After her death, things kicked into overdrive. We switched to health food almost exclusively. I don't mean sprouted grains and unbleached nuts. This was the '90s. Fat was the enemy, and I Can't Believe It's Not Butter! and Caffeine Free Diet Coke were king. "Health food" wasn't actually healthy. Of course, we didn't know that yet. Sugar-free cookies and low-fat pizzas were presented as the sensible alternative to fried zucchini, so that's what my family ate as we stared down a particularly stressful family medical history. A linkage was created in my mind: Good eating prevents death—with a rather loose definition of "good eating."

And it wasn't just my family cementing the need to monitor food intake and my outward appearance. That time on the farm when I was nine may have been the first time someone said "You're fat" directly to my face, but perceived imperfections were brought to my attention even sooner. Kids pointed out the flaws in my thighs or in the shape of my stomach—but not just kids. Strangers on the street and some of my friends' parents said awful things, too. I remember my best friend's mom once asking me if I felt comfortable wearing shorts next to her daughter's slenderer body. Maybe I was eight.

I had lived my childhood over a soundtrack of constant verbal reminders of my chubbiness. It was as if the rest of the world assumed I did not actually live within my own body and therefore was unfamiliar with its shape. I think folks half expected me to thank them for pointing it out. "I *do* have a puffier tummy than your child. Thank you for mentioning it while giving us a snack, mother of my best friend."

Also: If I'd been lined up next to all the children in the entire world, the first adjective that would have come to mind to describe me wouldn't have been "fat." Perhaps it would have been "American" or "white" or "sporty" or "tommish" or "be-eye-patched." But I think folks around me were not so much using their powers of observation for accuracy as they were generally noticing that I was not a delicate waif of a girl. I wasn't fat so much as I was a total fucking studmuffin. Hindsight's 20/20.

As adults, my sisters and I have almost identical body types, but as kids, my sister Allyson was all string and I was all bean. For years I had wanted to be spiky like her. I longed for sharp knees and painful-to-hug shoulders, and my ideal body type for myself was Ichabod Crane from Disney's animated *The Legend of Sleepy Hollow*.

My envy of Allyson began to reverse as she entered puberty. By thirteen, Allyson had already sprouted the famous Esposito family rack, and because we shared a bathroom and she had the modesty of a ballerina (none), I knew everything else involved in womanhood had kicked off for her, too. Where Allyson had turned into a full-on woman overnight, I was in the dirt-smudged boygirl zone of my youth and could have passed for a Lost Boy in any production of *Peter Pan*. I was an entire puberty behind Allyson with no ballerina vibes on my horizon. I could better relate to Britton, seven years younger than me, with whom I could still watch cartoons or dig holes in our backyard. But even Britton's body made me feel jealous: She was just one solid, tight muscle— a three-year-old with a six-pack.

I was a collection of loose ends—glasses, braces, eye patch, and my circular haircut that harkens to mind that container used to hold soup. Alone, each of these details would have been enough to tank my childhood social life. Together, they made me almost untouchable. It's tough to take a kid down a rung for having a coconut's hairdo when they're too cross-eyed to see the bottom of the ladder.

Trying out for my school's fifth grade volleyball team, I volleyed the ball directly into the rafters and a huge chunk of ceiling tile and construction dust fell on my head and I may have audibly farted in that moment and my peers were still basically like, "I dunno. Put her on the team." Either they had all seen *Carrie* too young and thought, "For fire safety, don't pick on the weirdest one," or there was a comfort in keeping someone around who just couldn't compete, at all, in terms of coolness. For whatever reason, I got a pass.

Then my pre–sixth grade summer hit.

It was pure makeover montage. What had formerly been a Swedish pancake (they're flatter than regular pancakes) chest became breasts, and I started growing hair on my legs. I snuck my mom's razor to shave it off and reclaim my youth, but after an hour in the bathtub only succeeded in making myself look *more* like a young woman. And so, I decided to do something to keep my body in check: I went on my first diet.

I was eleven.

Eleven is an awful age to begin dieting. The body is still growing, sexuality is emerging, and self-image and self-consciousness begin to solidify. We spend our childhoods coiling our self-hate, our adulthoods trying to unravel it, and our *Twilight* years trying to impregnate Bella and defeat the Volturi. Eleven is right in the midst of that coiling, when critical thinking becomes possible and we reason out the first supporting arguments for the lifelong thesis "Why I Suck: A Compendium." Eleven was the age my self-hatred became sentient and began to hunt John Connor. Up until that point, I was embarrassed of myself, but I wasn't yet aware of a way I could punish myself for being too weak or applaud myself for taking control.

I started by measuring my food before meals, weighing out portions on a tiny kitchen scale that my mom had from when she was trying to lose weight after being pregnant with Britton. Before long, I had memorized the calorie counts of different meats and starches. I tracked my intake and logged my portions. To this day, I know the calorie count in the recommended serving size of most foods.

This all happened during a very significant timeframe. Each summer, the new crop of sixth graders would hit Oakbrook Center mall to lurk near the Rock N Roll McDonald's, heave their pubescent chests at the heavens, and spray one another with various Bath & Body Works scents.

Fifth graders could not hang out at this mall. Fifth graders could Rollerblade to the Walgreens at the strip mall near the train tracks or walk to the public school, but only kids sixth grade and up could babysit and watch *Pretty Woman* and get dropped off at the fancy outdoor mall to roam a coed fog of hormones, because sixth grade marked the first year anyone in our class would become a teen. It was a ritual crossing of the River Styx but for sexual awakening.

Going to Oakbrook was such a rite of passage, we could have adopted it as regional period slang.

"Did you hear about Meghan?"

"No. What?"

"Over the weekend, she went to Oakbrook."

"Whoa! Did she say what it looks like? I've heard the color scheme's red and brown."

When I was dropped off at Oakbrook, it was as a Doc Martens sandals–wearing butterfly recently emerged from a bowl-cut-adorned chrysalis. I had grown my hair out, traded in my big red glasses for wire frames, gotten my braces off, and retired my eye patch. It was that classic Hollywood transformation where the girl has the eye patch and then she doesn't and she's suddenly hot. In my case, the "suddenly hot" was in fact the well-planned-out result of a seriously brutal summer. I'd lost about ten pounds—which is a lot when you don't yet weigh one hundred—and I had no plans to stop dieting.

Plus, I liked the new way I was treated. I got *ooh*s and *ahh*s from my classmates over my new body. I liked trying on my friends' clothes and finding the clothes were too big for me. I liked (erroneously) never worrying that the food I was—and wasn't—eating might kill me. Being tiny seemed to work better all around.

So I stopped eating butter. Cookies and pizza were cut out next; I didn't eat a cookie from the time I was in seventh grade until I went to college. By fourteen, I was getting ready to enter high school and eating only from a strict menu I devised myself in keeping with the low-fat faux health food craze. My preferred foods were pasta (cooked, no butter, no oil, no sauce), reduced-fat graham crackers, and soft-serve frozen yogurt from McDonald's. In the '90s, anything low-fat was fine. If I were a kid now, I would have probably been able to make more sensible choices, like consuming exclusively almonds and ice chips.

I reached my full height around fourteen, too—a towering five feet, four inches—and weighed about twenty-five pounds less than I do now, an unnatural weight for me. How do I know it was unnatural? By the way I maintained it. I set up a daily eating schedule and allowed no deviation from my planned eating for the day. Even a single bite I had not planned out would send me into a fury. I would scream at my parents, begging them to explain why they had given me the body I was born with. I would storm out of restaurants, unable to be around people who were breaking the arbitrary rules I had set for myself. When I started dating, I started binge eating because the whole experience made me feel so weird and stressed out and uncomfortable, totally messing up my calorie count and causing remorse for days.

I developed an aversion to chewing sounds that I still struggle with and would have to engage in a practice I termed "sensory deprivation"—plugging my ears and covering my eyes—to eat meals with my family or even watch someone eat a meal on television. I became so nervous about food that I began to have an exceptionally difficult time in the bathroom. My anxiety settled in my digestive tract and tore right through it. Either because the food I allowed myself was processed horsecrap or because eating caused me so much stress, I was no longer able to shit easily. I had debilitating stomach cramps and had to spend hours in the bathroom when I got home from school.

For all my anger and discomfort, I also felt intoxicating levels of self-satisfaction at changing the body I was so dissatisfied with through sheer force of will. I remember the joy I felt purchasing pants in a size 00—a size so small it is actually smaller than the smallest size! I was deeply occupied by counting ribs in the mirror, and spent nights lying in bed with my shirt pulled up, staring down at my concave stomach. An interesting inverse proportionality also began to take shape: the thinner I got, the more private I became about my body. The things I disliked about myself only stuck out in greater relief to the parts I began to obsess over. "I will show my body when it is perfect," I would tell myself, nibbling on an exact serving size of Goldfish crackers before heading off to the bathroom to spend the rest of my evening trying to shit.

It wasn't until college that I started to approach eating in a healthier way than planned starvation. It wasn't that I felt suddenly different about myself and then took actions to adjust my behavior—it was more the opposite; I was forced into very different eating circumstances, and almost accidentally changed my eating habits. Looking back, I feel like this could have just as easily gone the other way. Think of everyone eating and drinking indiscriminately and gaining the freshman fifteen. Being around so many people who were trying things for the first time, not really monitoring their eating, and also eating so publicly, there was something there that helped me let go of some of my unhealthy food-related patterns.

Without the same access to isolation and hiding that my disease thrived on, I started to get better. Still, it took me until my late twenties to identify these behaviors as disordered eating, and to realize they needed attention, even if the thought patterns may never be fully undone.

My compulsion can't be treated with abstinence; I have to eat to live. I do find honesty helps, as does shifting my focus to how my body feels instead of how my body looks, and that took work—therapy, reading, education, conversation. I sometimes fail to keep my focus on nutrition instead of "results." Eating can be exhausting. But I can eat on set and I can shit on a plane and I don't scream at my parents over food and I sometimes feel comfortable in my skin. So this is all to say: the *Comedy Bang! Bang!* set wasn't the first time I'd taken my shirt off in front of a woman or women—YOU KNOW IT WASN'T!—but it *was* a moment of victory for me. It was a little secret victory—a Victorious Secret— because I stood in my bra in front of a stranger and felt okay.

The bigger wins, though, are the moments when I stand in a bra (or braless) in front of a mirror or in the shower and think, *Fuck you, little boy on the dock when I was nine. I like how I look. My body is useful and my body is beautiful.* And of course, I won't be talking to that little boy on the dock. Or my family. Or other kids' parents. Or culture. I'll be talking to the person most critical of my body for the longest period of time: my own damn self.

SEX ED

Once I was in Chicago about halfway through an hour-long set and had just deftly transitioned from a hilarious bit about lesbian pornography into a series of jokes about the merits of butt sex when I heard a lady's voice yell out, "They didn't teach you *this* at Benet!"

Benet is the name of my high school, and even though this particular show was in my hometown, someone knowing I'd gone there and yelling at me about it was a surprise. We were at a low-ceilinged downtown comedy club, I was telling jokes that had nothing to do with high school, and I was solidly past the yell-the-name-of-your-high-school age. There are moments when heckling is better left unaddressed—say, at an outdoor music festival when the crowd could devolve into a Molly-fueled human centipede at any moment—and moments it cannot be ignored, like when the name of your far-suburban high school is inexplicably sandwiched into a perfect run of pro-butt-sex jokes.

I put my hand to my eyes to try to see under the lights and addressed the voice. "Did I go to high school with you, or were you my teacher?" The voice had sounded a bit older, like it definitely had stable insurance.

"Neither," she said. "We know your parents."

I didn't ask the woman's name. I moved on and finished my set. Whoever she was, she either desperately wanted some sex tips, or she desperately wanted to make sure I knew my parents would be getting a full report on my material, as if that might embarrass me. Please. With over a decade and a half of my comedy career behind me, my "we'll come to shows whenever you'll let us" parents had seen it all. The first time they came to see me do stand-up, the comic directly after me talked about pooping into his girlfriend's mouth. I was standing next to them as he went through the nature of their relationship and the texture of the poop, and I remember thinking, *Well, good. They're getting a real taste of my field.* ("Taste" probably wasn't the right word to use after a poo/mouth reference. Or was it exactly right?)

Benet Academy: that's the full name of the fancy-ass high school I attended. My older sister, Allyson, went there first and it didn't quite kill her, though its rigidity did turn my dorky bangs-and-glasses older sis into a sneaks-out-her-bedroom-window party girl. My parents firmly believed in the power of faith-based schooling, and just because they'd had to take Allyson's locked bedroom door off its hinges to see if she was inside each weekend didn't mean the plan should be altered. Man, I wish it had been. They sent us to Catholic school at the expense of retirement savings. In their late sixties, both my parents still work without plans to retire. My stupid private school education is part of what put them in that position, and I wish I could feel grateful but I just feel guilty, which I guess means Catholic school worked.

But not just Catholic school. An *academy*, for heaven's sake. The name alone makes it sound like an estate with a butler, or a guy who rows crew at Harvard. "That Benet Academy; what a cox-swain! Get him on the water if you can. By the way, how's it going with that new project of yours...what's it called...Facebook?"

Allyson graduated from Benet when I was in eighth grade, and by that time, I was already set to attend the following fall. Like I said, her high school experience was very "Girls Just Want to Have Fun"; she'd gone from shy bookworm ballerina to popu-lar pom-pom girl who danced at halftime shows and seemed to attract an endless string of male suitors. I'd gone to Benet for games and pep rallies many times during her four years to watch her perform and had felt like royalty. "You see that dancer with the ponytail that moves like an ad for ponies and tails? That's my sister." Her high school experience was exactly what I hoped for; I figured that if I went to Benet, I'd become wild and excit-ing, too.

Even so, I didn't know Allyson very well at the time. She kept a lot of her dating and social life secret and was always rushing out the door to parts unknown.

"That is nothing like high school," she called over her shoulder as she breezed off, curlers falling from her hair. I'd been watching *My So-Called Life*.

"Feels like high school to me," I called after, switching to *Doug* and beckoning Britton over to watch with me. That's one posi-tive thing about being in the middle: When your big sister is too grown-up to hang with you, you can be the cool big sis to your little sister. This probably makes being the littlest sister pretty difficult.

In fact, Britton may have ended up the raddest and most inde-pendent of the Esposito siblings. She lives in Argentina with her fiancé and is studying to be a doula. She moved to another continent alone, speaks Spanish fluently, and is the only person in my family who is bilingual. She is brave and strong and knows herself and I still constantly feel like I need to give her advice simply because I've been on the planet seven years longer. How annoying.

Back to Benet. The school is fifteen miles west of Western Springs in a suburb that recently transitioned from farming community to strip mall mecca. The property itself is a series of chilling redbrick buildings that were once home to an orphanage. Set back from the street at the end of a long, tree-lined driveway, the buildings are connected by warped, uneven staircases. Outside the school's main entrance and past the parking lot is a tiny cemetery of twenty child-size headstones, each weathered to the point of illegibility. Students believe these are the graves of children who died in a fire on-site. In my day, it was said that those children could sometimes be seen hovering alongside the statue of Mary, God's mom, positioned in the school's sole fourth-floor window. Just a few rusty turn-of-the-century gynecological tools and it would have been the set of *American Horror Story: College Prep*.

Want further horrors?

I took Religion right near that haunted Mary all four years. Never once saw a specter, but I did only have that class on alternate days to Physical Education. Monday/Wednesday/Friday we hung out near various unseen Caspers and read the Gospels or learned which Pope never decomposed after being buried (John XXIII). Tuesday/Thursday we roller-skated. We never confirmed that there was a fire on campus because the school library stocked absolutely zero books titled *Ghosts That Live Near Your Religion Classroom*. But even unconfirmed, we believed. We were Catholics; we took it on faith.

Academically, Benet was the second-strongest high school in the state at the time I went there. I got a solid, if not practical, education there. You were a failure if you didn't take a thousand AP classes and score well on the SAT and the ACT and memorize Shakespeare. Had I gone to the public school walking distance from my house, perhaps I'd have discovered some information about who I was or what I wanted to do for a living. Maybe I'd even have found out I liked being onstage.

As it was, I took a train thirty miles round-trip to Benet and but soft what light through yonder window breaks it is the east and Juliet is the sun arise fair sun and kill the envious moon who is already sick and pale with grief that thou her maid art far more fair than she and that's *Romeo and Juliet* from memory twenty years after I learned it so put that in your vape and smoke it.

The only sex ed with which I'd entered high school came from a harrowing cabin-in-the-woods experience with all the other girls in my class when I was ten. A nun walked into the cabin in full habit—that's one of those black-and-white numbers Whoopi Goldberg wears in *Sister Act*—went over to an old-school phonograph, and put the needle on the record. "Only the Good Die Young" by Billy Joel started playing. Right after the line "Catholic girls start much too late," the nun did a literal record scratch and then regarded us seriously. "That's what the world thinks of you," she said, pointing around at us. "They want to take your flower." On the word "flower," I felt in my pants what I thought was fear urine, so I went to the restroom—where I realized I had just gotten my first period. Bleeding in the middle of the woods, susceptible to bear attack, with the only potential source of aid being a scary-as-fuck nun, I went into survival mode, transferred the entirety of a roll of toilet paper onto my hand, shoved it into my pants, and carried on.

Tampons were a years-long struggle, since as a Catholic, you're not really supposed to root around down there. I definitely tried using tampons; I'd lock myself in the bathroom for hours at a time, unfurling the schematic that comes in the tampon box in an unsuccessful and vaguely scholarly attempt to figure out which holes were which and what exactly was going on down there. Rather than using an "aim and ease" method, though, I thought it was more about sheer force. You know how when you're on a drawbridge trying to break into a castle à la *Lord of the Rings*, you'll call for a battering ram that's an entire felled tree fitted with a fiery wolf head? That was more the technique I employed.

Besides Billy Joel being mad at me, I didn't learn anything else about sex until senior year at Benet, when it was sprinkled into our Religion class. There was no schlepping around a sack of flour to illustrate the responsibility of parenthood or putting a condom on a banana for practice. There was only labeling girls who so much as kissed multiple guys as "skanks" and ridiculing them as relentlessly as they were pursued.

Oh! And we watched a videotape of an abortion.

Did you read that right? *We watched a videotaped abortion. In class. As a course requirement.* The woman having the abortion was under local anesthesia only, and the camera was angled below her, looking up from under her vulva. The video was introduced as proof of the sinful, lonely, harrowing nature of abortion and was so graphic that any medical procedure—say, wisdom teeth being pulled—shot similarly could have been included in the *Saw* franchise.

It was well-known among students that every year several girls had abortions, and I cannot imagine what this was like for them—their teachers lecturing on the sinfulness of their personal, right-for-them decision to not become a parent as a teenager and then requiring that they watch the most extreme abortion footage possible for course credit. Those of us who hadn't had sex yet didn't fare much better. Creating a one-to-one linkage between sex and abortion in a high schooler's mind is like teaching driver's ed but only covering insurance premiums, collisions, and engine stalls. Yes, those things can be a part of driving, but driving's not all tough decisions and heavy maneuvers. Driving is also fun and useful and involves a bit of skill. Some people drive so well, they do it for a living.

We didn't listen to an embarrassing lecture about body hair or hear about any of the ways in which sex can be fun, useful, and skilled. We sat in class on a haunted fourth floor, surrounded by the ghosts of orphans born to unwed mothers, watching a medical procedure as shot by Alfred Hitchcock. The message was clear: The only way to prevent dying in an orphanage fire or starring in a vaginal horror film was to never have sex.

Especially gay sex.

After the abortion video, we read the Bible story about Sodom and Gomorrah aloud in class. If you've never read the story of Sodom and Gomorrah, it's not a clear condemnation of queerness. Townsmen in those cities try to rape angels and God has a problem with this. It could be, and has been, interpreted by

Biblical scholars as anti–sexual assault, not anti-gay. We didn't learn that. We learned that gays were definitely condemned to hell, a real place full of endless burning, and we were assigned a five-paragraph essay on the topic. I'm not being glib when I say that the most effeminate, gaydar-flagging men I knew at the time were priests, and one of them probably graded this paper.

I found my essay on a floppy disk a few years back. I wrote, *Since I am not gay, I don't know whether or not it is a choice and therefore cannot pass judgment.* About as progressive as I could possibly have been at the time. I'm sure I even felt proud of my open-mindedness as I turned in the paper before walking into the hall and saying, "That paper was gay." At Benet in 1999, "that's gay" was pretty much everyone's favorite insult. And if we felt like we did poorly on a gay paper, we said, "That raped me."

"How'd your paper go?"

"Gay. It raped me."

I said shit like that. Not the best, really.

So I guess what I'm building toward is: I REALLY wish I'd had sex ed. I wish we all had. Because, like many of you, I got around to having sexy feelings anyway. I just got there with absolutely no information about what to do about them.

I was fifteen when I first kissed a guy. I was over at my friend Barry's for a (gasp!) coed movie night—still a totally shocking event at that age. My best friend Gina and I had gone over together and she, along with everyone else for that matter, was visibly riled up to be sharing space with the opposite sex. The guys and gals were parked on either end of the basement waiting for some justifiable reason to get closer. We'd watched about twenty minutes of the movie when Barry suggested we mix things up.

"There's a small storage closet down here," he said. "If we go in and turn the lights off, it will be completely dark." It was an inspired suggestion. What better way to break the ice than cramming a dozen hormonal teens into a room the size of a wine fridge?

There was a particularly sweet and sensitive guy with us in the basement that night, and I had heard he had a crush on me. And honestly, I liked a lot of things about him: He had these huge, beautiful hands, played bass in a ska band, and had a close relationship with his sister. He was a real best-friend-Julia-Roberts-realizes-she-has-feelings-for type. I should also say: Sexuality is a spectrum. This is true even if you are a lesbian-y lesbian's lesbian. I think dicks are chill, whoever's body they may be on, and I wouldn't kick Jason Momoa's brand of Aquaman out of my ocean. I can imagine having straight sex, though I'm not totally sure I've ever actually had it (we'll come back to that). All of that said, when I'm with men, I can never quite relax. My relationships with dudes never felt as deep or intimate as the ones I've had with women and nonbinary folks.

Smashed against all the other kids in that storage room, I could feel someone gently ease their way beside me. Most fifteen-year-old boys are not exceedingly gentle; I knew it had to be Bass Boy.

So when he reached over and took my hand in the pitch dark, I instantly recognized it was him and I squeezed his in return. He took a side step and turned his body just a bit. I could feel his breath on my forehead. Then I felt his lips on mine. His lips were nice—all ChapSticked up for the occasion—and we held the kiss for a moment. Then Barry yelled out, "Someone is kissing in here! I can hear their mouth noises!" The light was flipped on and we were caught, the witnesses cementing the fact that not only had

Bass Boy been my first kiss, but also that my first kiss literally happened in the closet.

All bets were off after that. Kids filed out of the storage room, paired off, and went to different corners of the basement. Light make-outs ensued across the board. An hour later our parents picked us up. On the phone that night, Gina dug for information. "Do you like him?" she asked. "Are you going to date him?"

I said, "Yes, I like him," because there wasn't anything else to say. I did like him. I supposed that meant I should date him. So I did.

But Bass Boy wasn't my high school boyfriend. That relationship lasted about six months. Then I was single for maybe a day and a half before Nate asked me out. Nate was our class's Archie Andrews, the pumped-up version from *Riverdale*, not the scrawny, pointillist-drawn Double Digest version from my youth. Nate had been the star of Benet's varsity football team since sophomore year, when he was the only underclassman playing varsity. He played offense, defense, and special teams. In the spring, he ran anchor leg on the school's 4×100-meter relay team even though he wasn't on the track team. He'd just show up for meets and win.

He looked about thirty, like an adult actor playing a teen. You know that one guy in your class who developed early? The dude with pecs and a deep voice who made Channing Tatum's character in *21 Jump Street* seem believable? That was Nate. Hanging out with him was like spending time with a velvet painting of a stallion or a wax sculpture of Brad Pitt in *Troy* that really wanted to take me to Applebee's.

I didn't date Nate because of how he looked, though. He was kind, gentle, soft-spoken with me and loud and fun with his friends. He always finished his homework a day early, sang along when I played John Denver, deferentially called my dad "Mr. Esposito" even after my dad told him, "Call me Nick," and listened so intently anytime Britton described the plot of a *Rugrats* episode that he'd ask follow-up questions. When I took him to see *The Blair Witch Project*, got scared, accused him of being "in on it," and refused to allow him back in my car for a ride home, he didn't get mad. "I'm not a witch, but I'll call my dad for a ride, Cammy." He called me Cammy, the first and only person to do so before I started calling myself that on podcasts and Twitter and in the second person when walking around my apartment alone.

If anything, his body threw me off. He was so perfectly muscled and utterly proportional that it made me jealous. At night, in my dreams, I looked like that, too. Externally, and to the rest of the world, however, I did not. I was in possession of two ever-growing breasts, which even then had just a few stretch marks, and muscular but dimpled-by-cellulite thighs. I had a totally normal bod, even if ads for razors didn't make me feel that way, but it wasn't the bod I imagined myself having. If he was K. J. Apa's Archie Andrews, I was the lovably awkward extra who accidentally looks directly into the camera so they have to shoot the whole scene again.

For starters, I was my school's mascot—a giant red bird. When Nate would score a touchdown, I'd run up and down the sidelines waving an enormous *B*-emblazoned flag and flapping my bird arms to indicate the appropriate number of points. Classic high school couple. Having school uniforms probably saved me some major social face, but I was never able to catch up to Allyson's femininity. In fact, my girlishness seemed to decrease by the year. I'd begun my freshman year with shoulder-length hair, a plaid uniform skirt, white knee-high socks, and loafers, but by sophomore year and Nate, my hair barely hit my chin. I wore two thick beaded chokers, navy blue boot-cut khakis, and white platform steel-toed Doc Martens boots, and had a black eye for all of spring semester because I took a nap next to a pool table.

Technically, this broke our dress code, but I was a Student Government representative, altar server, and retreat leader. The key to never getting in trouble at our school was to be over-the-top involved on campus; it'd be impossible for any faculty member to fault someone who spent their free time leading prayer vigils and planning pep rallies. Which would be a brilliant and devious strategy, except that I was doing them because I genuinely loved all these things. Where Catholicism met activism: This was my sweet spot.

There's a left-wing part of Catholicism—liberation theology— that's all about justice and Cool Jesus. Cool Jesus is a socialist. Cool Jesus is friends with the poor. He hangs with sex workers. He's out there with the masses. Cool Jesus is going to overthrow the man. He comes into temples and flips tables. Cool Jesus was my Jesus. Catholicism was just a punk rock way of making social change happen, and I was very, very into it. In my Docs.

Maybe there was some subconscious part of me that felt like I could wear whatever I wanted in high school because I had clear evidence of my straightness in my Hemsworth-brother boyfriend. Our relationship granted me leeway to be myself.

One time during senior year, I got to fly extra close to his hypermasculine sun. We had a school dance that was famous couples themed, and—having literally been voted Couple Most

Likely to Live Happily Ever After by our graduating class—we went to the dance dressed as each other. He donned nylons, a wig, and this T-shirt I wore to cheer for him at road games when I wasn't suited up as the bird. I wore his football uniform. It was my favorite dance. I had the time of my life. Not because I was with my boyfriend, but because—for the night—I got to *be* my boyfriend *and* date a girl. Confusingly, that girl was another version of me. Very *Inception*, right? Dating a me within a him? By the way, I hate that movie. It makes me cold.

Nate never pressured me for sex. When I told him my friends said he definitely masturbated because all boys masturbated, he insisted, "I don't." He was more than a good guy; he was a good CATHOLIC guy. And good Catholic guys are supposed to wait.

There was comfort in his "good guy" waiting, because I wanted to wait, too. At school, I was an outspoken advocate of abstinence. I never shamed anyone for their choices, but I felt it was my duty to confirm my virginity to my classmates. "We're waiting," I'd say, completely unaware that waiting to have sex was supposed to be hard. Well, I knew it was supposed to be *hard*, but I didn't know it was supposed to be *difficult*—that some of my classmates had an actual urge to have sex. The way I figured it, Catholics didn't have sex before marriage. I was such a good Catholic, I didn't even *want* to.

I didn't realize that I could *want* to have sex. I didn't have a sex life with myself—I certainly didn't masturbate. My limitations were so extreme that I had rules set up about how and when Nate and I could make out. Things like: "You can never kiss my right shoulder," and, "No hand holding during *Dawson's Creek* as it might cut the tension and ruin the watching experience." You know, normal rules that all teen girls enthusiastically maintain in the face of raging hormones.

Even those rules didn't protect me from the utter disgust I'd feel every time we kissed. Let me be clear: The kissing felt good. Generally, if you are a human being—and I believe you probably are, unless the machines have taken over—kissing feels good. There's closeness and acceptance and arousal built into the act of placing your lips against another person's. It's a special, private thing. I wasn't disgusted with Nate. I was disgusted with myself. Nothing about my body felt right to me, even after all the massively unhealthy steps I'd taken to transform my body type from rectangle to stick. I had the flat stomach and tiny ass I'd been starving for, but hoped to keep both to myself indefinitely.

It was during high school that I started having sex dreams about women. I don't think I chalked it up to anything at the time. If you walked into my bedroom, there was a giant poster of Alicia Silverstone as Batgirl over my bed, a big shot of Claire Danes as Angela Chase, and torn-out pages of girls from magazines all over my walls. Men had been relegated to the back of my door, which I'd wallpapered in tiny, two-inch cut-out heads of dude celebrities, all smashed together. It looked like a collage they'd find on *True Detective* when it was the sweet, studious teen who'd boiled the skin off those skulls all along.

I did try to have sex with Nate one time, when we first went off to college. We didn't go to the same school; he was several hours south in Washington, DC, playing football for a college known for its academics. He couldn't leave campus during football season, so I surprised him for a long weekend our freshman year. I took a train overnight from Boston to DC and then caught a cab to his town house. I rang the bell and greeted him with what I assumed any college football player would want from his girl-friend: a big bear hug and a pat on the butt. He left for practice and I slept for a bit, then waited anxiously for his return. I think I even did his dishes.

Keep in mind that the extent of my sexual education at this point was misguided tampon-cramming, a Halloween horror movie on abortion, and whatever I could glean from *Dirty Dancing*, which is also technically a movie about abortion, although a better one. One or two of my friends had had sex at some point during high school, and the rest of us were virgins. Which, by the way, what is virginity? 'Cause if I never had sex with a man, would that make me a virgin? I'd never gone to a gynecologist. I vaguely thought it might be possible to get pregnant from giving a blow job. Not that I gave blow jobs. I, in fact, most certainly did not.

During one of the final games of our senior year of high school, Nate scored six touchdowns and rushed for over four hundred yards. For non-football-heads, that's like a gold medal amount. After his sixth run into the end zone, a friend turned to me. *"Now will you give him a blow job?!"* she screamed, accidentally timing her yell so that the roaring crowd had just died down.

And I honestly believe a lot of the parents sitting near us in the stands agreed. *Yes*, their eyes seemed to suggest, *you really should. It's the least you could do.* Mind you, I don't think any of the women on our basketball team were offered sexual rewards for almost winning state that year, but that's because it's different for boys. Boys need to get blow jobs or their genitals will pack up and leave their bodies. That's a fact.

That night I broke rule #72—"No mouths on things that aren't mouths"—and gave a very societally pressured blow job. Or most of one. A little bit of semen's road opener hit the back of my throat at the exact moment that I needed to sneeze. If you've never had pre-cum shoot out your nostrils, I'll tell you this: It burns quite a bit. I leaned against a lit Weber grill at my sixth-grade birthday party and gave myself second-degree burns on my leg but had to pretend that was fine and stay at the party because sixth grade is brutal. Splooge in the nose kind of feels like that but without the staying at the party. As I flushed my nose out with water, I kindly explained to Nate that God clearly didn't want me breaking rule #72. "You saw what happened!" I said. "This was essentially a medical emergency, so bjs must be unholy." He rolled over and finished things himself before never bringing it up again.

Anyway, I went to visit Nate at the very beginning of college, and when he got home I proposed a plan: "We will have sex today!" We walked hand in hand to the nearest convenience store to buy condoms. The most direct route to the store involved taking an especially perilous and terrifying set of stairs, the same stairs used in the filming of *The Exorcist*. They are steep as fuck. You know when the priest gets thrown down the stairs at the end of *The Exorcist* and you're like, "That's an especially perilous and terrifying set of stairs. Those are steep as fuck!" It was those stairs. The whole time down I worried I would fall to my death and someone would have to tell my mother, "She was out buying condoms and those stairs, they kill priests. You think they're gonna tolerate some floozy who planned to have responsible, protected sex?"

When we got to the convenience store, Nate went inside alone and I stayed outside under the streetlamps looking like a total midnight creep. He came back out utterly defeated, saying, "They're out of condoms."

"What do you mean they're out of condoms?" I said. "That's not a thing. We just need like one condom. Go get one condom!"

He shrugged. "They're out."

So we went back to his place and tried to improvise. We got naked and he generally rubbed his private parts near and around my private parts; we essentially wrestled in the true Greco-Roman style. I stayed for the weekend and we ate lots of pancakes. He asked a teammate for some condoms and we sort of used them but more in a scientific, exploratory way. Sunday evening, I got on a train back to Boston, completely unsure of whether I had lost my virginity and not entirely invested either way. Nate and I broke up not long after, although not because I noticed my total disinterest in men—yet.

During high school, when Nate and I would get off the phone at night or when he'd gone home after a hangout, I'd need hours to unwind from the experience. Alone, I'd sit at my parents' kitchen table, stress-eating bowl after bowl of Kix—perhaps the first thing I'd eaten all day—and try to block out the memory of his touch. To do so, I'd think of my best friend, Gina, and wonder what she was doing. It never occurred to me that this might mean something.

FIRST LOVE

I met Gina freshman year of high school and because of her, joined the swim team. Like Nate, she was a natural athlete—almost six feet tall, muscular and broad-shouldered with an admirable ease to her gait and a commanding presence. She was the kind of person you'd assume could bow hunt, or at least handle herself around large snakes. A real *Xena: Warrior Princess* type, except she had eyes that looked perpetually sleepy. Her vibe was "I can hog-tie any of you as soon as I wake up from this nap." She was slow as a sloth on land but a beast in the water, really fucking fast with minimal effort.

Unlike Nate, she was a rascal. Not un-Catholic or anything. She went to Mass every Sunday with her family and was also planning to wait until marriage to have sex. But she cursed with ease! She drove a white Audi convertible totally inappropriate to the Chicago climate! She owned leather pants, and sometimes, she wore them!

I might not have even stayed on the swim team were it not for five a.m. practice with Gina and the breakfast we'd share afterward. Leaving my house at four thirty a.m. to go jump in a pool on a freezing-cold October morning never appealed to me on its own. But the time I'd get to spend with Gina definitely did. Post-practice we'd go to McDonald's. Gina would get the full breakfast:

pancakes, eggs, and orange juice. I'd get my twist cone. We'd sit alongside the other early-morning McDonald's patrons—a predictable group of maybe seven single men in their early eighties each sitting alone at a table—and gab about whose backstroke had improved and which LeAnn Rimes songs ruled. It was bliss.

Of course, because nothing is fair, it was me, not her, who was elected swim team captain our senior year. It wasn't because I was a particularly good swimmer. I was a three-sport athlete— swim team in the fall, basketball in the winter, and soccer in the spring—but I was not naturally athletic. I just had a lot of energy. In a way, I played "personality sports"—making cuts because I launched my body with reckless abandon, wore garish sweatbands, and generally brought a bit of pizzazz to the team. I believe this is generally referred to as "playing with heart," and I had heart to spare.

For instance, at the end of my sophomore year in high school, I injured my knee playing soccer. I had to have surgery and spend the summer in a giant knee brace. I didn't do a damn thing to stay in shape that summer, though I did learn how to play "Amazing Grace" and nothing else on the guitar and how to hop a fence when your friends are hopping a fence but you can't bend your knee. When I went back out for the swim team the next year, I got cut because I was so slow, I was basically swimming backward. But I didn't let that deter me. No, I made a deal with the coach: Keep me on for a month, and I'll cut my time in half. I did double practices, and made the team—and I was *still* in the slowest lane. That's when I got captain. I guess my teammates were just like, "Aw...look at that little floater!" As captain, I spent my time sneaking out of every practice to take an hour-long shower instead of doing laps, before sliding into the water and finishing the last laps at full speed. I can't explain exactly why this was funny at the time, because now it only sounds obnoxious, but my teammates laughed and laughed.

There's a particular torture in being a young, closeted-to-yourself lesbian and a member of the swim team. It was a testament to my drive to be close to Gina that I was able to stay on the swim team and grit my teeth through the daily chest-kick that was spending time in the women's locker room directly before and after practice. At the time, I couldn't for the life of me figure out why the locker room made me lose my mind. Upon reflection, the answer is TOTAL NUDITY.

You know how bra wearers can change from a regular bra into a sports bra without removing our shirts? (We learn in sixth grade by osmosis and we get so good at it, we could be wearing suits of armor and still T-shirt-cannon our bras out the mouths of our helmets.) That's not what a swim team locker room is like. It's like walking into a scene from *Porky's*, a pervy, not-quite-porn film my guy friends loved to watch in high school. For the record, the first actual porn I saw was *Edward Penishands*, but that wasn't till college.

You see, gals don't wear bikinis or loose-fitting jerseys to swim team practice. They wear one-piece Speedos, specifically one-piece Speedos four sizes too small in order to cut down on drag in the water. A Speedo that tight cannot be wiggled into under a T-shirt or while wearing underwear or a bra. It cannot. To get into such a bathing suit a swimmer must first remove every stitch of clothing she is wearing and probably also some she has worn in the past. After she is all the way, *Orange Is the New Black*–shower-scene naked, the swimmer must then peel the suit up her body like so much sausage casing. Legs are lifted and thighs crammed into a square inch of Lycra fabric. Breasts are cradled and placed gently in a symmetrical position. I've seen less bod from partners I've lived with.

I never stared. Every queer human raised female, whether aware of her queerness yet or not, knows not to stare at other women in the locker room. We're women ourselves; we know what it's like to feel the daggers of an unwanted stare, and we don't put our friends through that. That's what posters of Alicia Silverstone and Claire Danes are for. Still, the notion that I'd be able to avert my eyes from three dozen teammates changing at once was preposterous, like going on a walk outside and trying not to look at the sky, if the sky was totally your type.

I'd be talking to someone about our English homework and suddenly she'd be au naturel. If there was an Oscar for maintaining deliberate eye contact in the face of harrowing nudity, Anne Hathaway would have won, because wow, she's such a terrific actor. But I would have been nominated. I focused my energy into not checking them out with the fire of a thousand averted-eyed suns, my entire body beet red from exertion, muttering Nate's name repeatedly under my breath like the beads of a straightness-inducing rosary. It was at *least* as good a workout as practice itself.

With Gina it was easier. She was my best friend. I didn't stare at her because I didn't need to. I saw her all the time: at practice, at school, and on the insides of my eyelids when I closed my eyes. Female best friendships are designed to be close; there's even societal pressure to have that one best friend who knows all of you. I could have read all the *Cosmopolitan* magazines in the world and it never would have seemed odd to me that I knew the exact chisel of her jaw and used the broad span of her shoulders as my standard form of measurement. "That place? Oh, it's a few hundred ginashoulderswidths down the road."

Gina was from a wealthy family. My parents' adorable four-bedroom house felt Barbie Dreamhouse–sized compared to her parents' sprawling mansion with several wings, a projection-screen TV, and backyard hot tub grotto. I slept over at her place often. She was one of ten kids and most of her older siblings had already left the house. There were seven empty bedrooms and two guest bedrooms in her home. Still, I insisted on sleeping in bed with her. I remember a night when her mother came in to check on us.

"You sure you want to sleep in here, Cameron?" her mom asked. "We literally have nine other empty beds you can sleep in."

My much-too-loud, much-too-quick response: "SHUT THE DOOR!"

All throughout high school, I was busy trying to spend as much time as possible with Gina. I'd go on vacations with her family. (I never went on a vacation with Nate's family, by the way.) If she was sad, I'd drive to her house and leave a Snickers on her windshield, where it would quickly melt into an oozy pile not unlike my heart. For her sixteenth birthday, I saved up for months to buy her a $200 pair of Guess jeans because I knew that's what she wanted. I think her boyfriend got her a flower.

One pivotal night we had a big sleepover with our core group of five female friends: the Dancer, the Joker, Second in Command,

Gina, and me. None of us were drinkers, but the Joker's parents were out of town, so we raided their liquor cabinet and found the hard stuff—a single bottle of green-apple-flavored schnapps, which we proceeded to split five ways. Predictably, we got first-time hammered and to this day I cannot have a single schnapp. Unpredictably, given Benet's explicit "no thanks to queerness" stance, once drunk, my friends started making out with each other.

Contrary to what Mike Pence, who as governor created an HIV epidemic in southern Indiana by defunding Planned Parenthood, may tell you, fear of sex can make friendships the easiest place to explore sexuality—especially for young women. I'm not totally sure what was going on for my friends at that time, but I didn't know people with vaginas could have orgasms until I helped cause one for someone else. Now I masturbate all the time. I'm doing it right now and that's why my keyboard is so sticky.

My upbringing may be *slightly* on the extreme side with regard to what I was taught about my own body (nothing), but it's not like many people raised female in American culture are taught to connect with our sexualities in a positive way. We don't even have a universally accepted slang term for masturbation if what you've got is a vagina. What I gleaned from culture about sex was that I was supposed to derive all my sexual pleasure from the achievement of making my boyfriend ejaculate using my beach body and these ten surefire methods. And that's what it was like as a part-nered individual. I can't even imagine being a single teen gal and having sexual urges. What are you supposed to do? Pretend hot tub jets do nothing for you?

Then you have these very intense friendships with other girls and there's a blurry feeling of almost wanting to *be* each other—this sense that everyone seems to have it better than you: Their skin is clearer, they have a smaller waist, their boyfriend is more interesting, their hair is prettier. You want to inhabit one another and that can have a sort of sexy vibe. That's what the movie *Wild Things* is about. Also *All About Eve*. But in *Wild Things* they actually kiss, which is why I own three copies.

The four other women hanging around this particular night were my CREW. We sat at the same lunch table at the cafeteria all four years. We left notes in each other's lockers, slipping them in through the little slots at the top that I think are air holes for the kids who get stuffed in there. We made plans to hang out every weekend; we went to dinner together, with our dates, before school dances. We had a favorite dean who let us cut class and cry in her office if we all had a fight, and we regularly flipped each other's uniform skirts up so the whole hallway or classroom could see our friend's underwear. Did we love or hate each other?

Both.

At this schnappsy sleepover, there was a pattern to who would kiss who. The friend group was structured thus: Gina was the Supreme Boss, and Second in Command and I were always vying for the Assistant to the Boss position in a platonic love triangle situation. The Joker and the Dancer were funny and artsy, respectively, and best pals with each other. So the two best friend duos paired off in the making out. I hoped I might automatically be paired off with Gina, but she went with Second in Command. After a few minutes, the friends switched, so the Joker was now with Gina and the Dancer was kissing Second in Command. I just stood there silently watching, paralyzed, continuing to not be kissed.

Honestly, I wish I'd had popcorn to cram in my face so I could at least have appreciated the cinematic beauty of the moment. Then we all went to bed, naked, in like, one bed I think? I lay there completely still, staring at the ceiling. Which, by the way, was a very familiar sleepover feeling for me, as everyone always wanted to watch *Se7en* and then snooze peacefully while I shook in my sleeping bag, thinking about that one scene with all the tree-shaped air fresheners.

Everyone told their boyfriends about it except me. When Nate eventually found out through the grapevine, he asked me if I was bisexual. I said I wasn't. I think my friends told their boyfriends because to them, it was this silly thing—but to me, even as a non-participant, it was real, and it would have been cheating if I'd done it. I guess that's what Nate sensed. Or maybe for one clairvoyant moment he realized that I, his very straight, not-even-a-little-bit-bi-or-anything-else girlfriend, had begged his younger brother to steal a very large poster of Angelina Jolie in *Girl, Interrupted* from the multiplex where he worked. Who knows.

After I basically told him, "No way, no gay!" Nate and I kept dating. At senior prom, he peeled off his sweaty-from-dancing tux shirt to reveal a white tank top upon which he had Sharpied *Cammy 4 Eva*. The night was wrapping up when pre-Trump-endorsing Shania Twain's "You're Still the One" came on over the crappy hotel ballroom speakers and I broke eye contact with Nate, sweet sporty Nate, and looked over at Gina, dancing nearby with her boyfriend.

When Gina and I locked eyes, I mouthed, "It's our song!" because it was. Nate and I moved closer, so we were positioned directly next to them, and I bid high school goodbye rocking back and forth, hands on my boyfriend's shoulders, staring into the face of my first love.

GOTTA HAVE FAITH, FAITH, FAITH

Not too long ago I was doing stand-up at the Upright Citizens Brigade Theatre in Los Angeles when I mentioned attending a college in Boston where it sucked to realize I was gay. After the show, another comic on the lineup asked if I was talking about Boston College. I said yes, and she yelled over to a group of her friends, who were in town to attend a bachelorette party in the desert and had gone to BC, too. Now, this comic is a woman of color, as was everyone in her group of friends, and BC is a pretty white school. Didn't take long till we were all screaming our respective grievances together in the lobby of this theater with such vigor that even though I ran a weekly show there, the box office attendee had to kick us out before we disturbed the *yes and* of whatever group was onstage at that moment.

Before we got kicked out, this other comic posed a very good question: "How the hell did you end up at BC? That place was homophobic as hell."

Welp, as seniors at Benet, many of my classmates and I eyed schools in Illinois, Indiana, and Ohio. University of Illinois, Northwestern, Miami University in Ohio, and Notre Dame were all pretty popular choices among my peers. Allyson had gone to Miami, an eight-hour drive from Chicago, and her number one piece of advice to me when I was applying to colleges was "Get the fuck out of the Midwest." Let me be clear: We love the Midwest. Midwest Is Best. I think she meant, "Try living somewhere else with different norms and weather and locally famous sandwich types (cheesesteak, Italian beef, Reuben, banh mi, etc)." I essentially decided where to apply based on what I'd seen emblazoned on those white hats with lines above and below the college name that were popular in the late '90s/early 2000s. Boston College was a hat I'd seen.

Besides hats, I got in with a little scholarship and fourteen other people in my class also decided to go there, so I chose BC.

When I graduated from Benet, I only knew that BC was for Catholic people who were also smart-ish. Benet was very specifically college-prep focused; the goal was to get into the highest-ranked college you could. We memorized the *U.S. News and World Report* rankings and were VERY COMPETITIVE with each other, which led to me and all 350 of my fellow classmates trying to collect accolades like so many Pokémon. If you were serious about your future, you were at least a twelve-sport athlete, chaired the French Club and were French but actually American because this is the USA goddamnit, organized clothing drives and religious retreats, and never, ever slept or left the school grounds for even five minutes to be a normal person—and I was serious about my future. So was everyone else, and for that reason, all of our applications were identical. That could be why fifteen of us ended up at BC.

The summer after graduating high school I was a lifeguard at an indoor pool, which felt right for my level of self-perceived sexiness. No tan. No waves. But one time I gave a kid a Band-Aid 'cause he hit his toenail on the waterslide.

Nate was working construction and getting ready to report early for pre-season training despite the fact that he fucked up his shoulder playing all positions, all four years. Football got him an education he probably couldn't have afforded or accessed otherwise. He essentially sold his body to be able to attend. His construction shifts were early in the morning; my lifeguard shifts were usually in the afternoon. We saw less of each other and still I couldn't imagine leaving him, going to a different college, meeting different people.

"Who will ever replace you?" I sobbed into his chest, hitting replay on the Céline Dion song that best fit the moment (this was the whole summer, so we probably used 'em all).

"You won't have to," he answered. "We'll stay together. I didn't write 'Cammy 4 Eva' on a tank because I thought this was short-term. By the way, should I also get that tattooed on my chest?"

I'm not sure if that dialogue is 100 percent correct, but he did want to get that tattoo.

In August, he and his dad pulled their family van out of the driveway to make the trip from Chicago to Washington, DC, and drop him off at school, and sometime around then I got a letter with my assigned dorm room on it. In the space where there was supposed to be the name and phone number of my incoming roommate, there was instead a blank nothing. Remember my crossed eyes? I didn't know it, but my parents had written BC a letter explaining that I had a medical condition that required uninterrupted sleep—which was true; my eyes would cross if I was tired. Still, A LITTLE MUCH, Mom and Dad! As a result, I was going to be my own roommate and live in one of two single rooms on the entire freshman campus, a converted maintenance closet in which they'd installed a window, which is nicer than Harry Potter ever got on Privet Drive.

So a few weeks after Nate and his dad left, my own dad and I pulled out of our driveway in the family van and hightailed it to Boston, arriving seventeen hours later because my dad doesn't stop for anything but peeing. BC is built into the side of a massive hill and freshmen live at the very top, I assume because we would be most overwhelmed by everything college-y happening around us, and could therefore roll to class if necessary. Well, some freshmen also live a bus ride away on the law school campus, but I wasn't one of those weirdos, thank god. I mean, this was before *Legally Blonde* came out. We were afraid of lawyers then.

I moved into my room alone. Well, my dad carried in the mini-fridge and the TV/VCR.

"You're the most Catholic person I know, Cameron. Don't leave your sisters behind."

And then he was gone.

I'd never been alone in my life, not for a second. Until four years prior, Allyson had been just across the hall in her room. After she left for college, Britton and I used to knock "Shave and a Haircut" on the shared wall between our bedrooms every night before going to sleep. My parents had been VERY involved in my life. My sisters were VERY loud. My boyfriend was VERY available. My friends were VERY sometimes mean to me but around a lot. I was a busy high schooler, all churchy and sporty. And now it was quiet.

I loved it.

I turned off the ringer on the phone—a landline that only my parents and sibs had the number to—and spent my first night rereading *The Catcher in the Rye*, my favorite book, which is a less ridiculously trite and twee favorite book if you're a woman. I basically never turned that ringer back on. Away from my loud and so-involved-with-each-other family, I LIVED IT UP, coming and going at ALL HOURS but especially REALLY EARLY IN THE MORNING when I'd wake up to go to Mass, where I was a Eucharistic minister (the person who gives you that little wafer of Jesus body) before class.

A lot of times when folks go to college, they reinvent or find themselves. For example, before college they were just a guy in the marching band but in college they become a guy in the marching band *with a goatee*. If you attended college, I'm likely envious of the trying-on of identities you did during those years. You arrived on campus one way and then found a new you that everyone got to meet and love or hate or love to hate. Maybe you bought a *Scarface* poster or maybe you started listening to jam bands or maybe you got involved in bringing freedom to Tibet. For me, I started college Catholic and, over the course of freshman year, got Catholic-er (not to be confused with Catholiquor, a term I just made up for the wine turned into Jesus's blood at Mass).

There's an element of Catholic schooling that feels very assembly-line-esque, and that's because it is a for-real Catholic factory. For all you non-Catholics out there, CONGRATS and have you ever worn a plaid uniform skirt? Because I have. Many times. And in a less sexy way than Britney Spears in "Baby One More Time" but in a more sexy way than Megan Fox in *Jennifer's Body*, because in that movie she eats human flesh and that's not sexy.

In Catholicism, there are seven sacraments you do while

wearing a white dress, and usually before you're old enough to understand them. You've definitely heard of some of them. First there's baptism. You're usually a baby when that happens. Someone pours water on your head to wash away Original Sin and you're saved from damnation phew, 'cause in Catholicism you're born sinful. The only person born without Original Sin was Mary, Jesus's mom, which is called the Immaculate Conception, a phrase a lot of folks think applies to Jesus's conception, but it doesn't. That's the Virgin Birth, when she was made pregnant without her consent and without ever having sex and an angel was her Clearblue Easy, appearing to tell Mary she was with child. Get your shit straight.

Anyway, babies who die without having water poured on their heads used to go to a place called Limbo, which was between heaven and hell and Catholics left on Earth could pray for those babies and move them from Limbo to heaven, until 2007 when the Church said, "Actually, Limbo doesn't exist." And if you are confused or upset by anything I've said in the past two paragraphs, imagine being seven years old and learning all this.

That's one reason I go to therapy.

Around second grade comes first communion, which is when you eat a little cracker the priest gives you because it's made of Jesus. I lined up alongside my classmates and said, "Yes. I believe this Triscuit-type thing is the flesh of that man whose bloody statue is hanging up there on the wall." I remember thinking it needed ketchup.

Next up is reconciliation, which is when you go into a small box or closet and explain your sins to a priest who is listening through a curtain. We did that in fourth grade, because ten-year-olds need to stop getting away with so many terrible, terrible sins for Christ's sake. And finally, there's confirmation, when you pick a name of some saint, learn about their miracles and horrifying death, and then become an adult in the Church. I did that in seventh grade, which you may recall wasn't the best decision-making age for me as I simultaneously attempted to starve myself into near-nonexistence, but hey, a shit-ton of saints did that, too, they just called it "fasting."

Dang if I don't think about being a kid and zooming through first communion, reconciliation, and confirmation like that was what all tiny human beings are doing. These weren't extracurriculars. They were a huge part of my daily schooling. The same people who taught me two plus two equals four also taught me to identify my sinfulness, feel shame about it, and turn to the Church as my only comfort.

I live in Los Angeles now and Scientology is everywhere here. My dog, Murph, regularly pees in front of Scientology's film studio, and I used to host a stand-up show every Tuesday night directly across from their "Celebrity Center." When Lawrence Wright's *Going Clear* published, it felt like everyone behind me in line at a coffee shop was saying, "Scientology is a scam and a cult and a cash grab and a scary organization that treats its members with cruelty" into some Bluetooth device. I believe all that.

And I believe I was raised in a church that has used time and college football to normalize the weird beliefs and traditions you just read about.

I'll never be without my upbringing in the Church. It's just in me. And I've been trying to figure out how to express it since childhood—like being a Eucharistic minister in college, which by the way didn't make me a loser or weirdo at BC. Sure, the majority of my classmates weren't going to Mass before class, but many of the students had chosen BC because it was Catholic and it was accepted to be a person of faith there, and even better to be a person of acts.

I wanted to become a priest, and being a Eucharistic minister is the closest you can get to being a priest if you're a woman. I mean, you can be a nun if you're a woman. But nuns don't get to stand on the stage, er, altar, and talk to the congregation about their opinions. Stand-up comics do, though.

BTdubs, I loved connecting with people at Mass. Talking with people about what matters in the world is my whole thing. It's the same reason I loved solidarity trips. What's a solidarity trip? It's when a bunch of my fellow students and I would spend a spring break building houses, holding the hands of the sick, praying in other people's churches, and then go back to the very expensive private schools that our parents were paying for. Looking back now, we were not the most helpful resource that could have been provided to a developing community—maybe they could have used a plumber or city planner or fair elections instead of poverty tourism for credit.

At the time, I felt helpful and went every chance I could. During my senior year of high school, for example, I led a solidarity trip to Appalachia. I'd gone home from school and said, "Mom, I need money because I'm going to visit these very sad people in this very sad area." As you may recall, my mom is actually from Appalachia. She donated and added, "You know I'm donating money to people who are living in very similar houses and conditions to where I grew up, right? These could be your relatives. They could be you."

I probably said, "Well, not *really* me." Because the focus of these trips wasn't so much "humans are all alike" as "Catholic teenagers are a little bit better than everyone else." And I did feel good about myself.

Every senior at Benet had the chance to go on this big weekend retreat. It was called Kairos and we started hearing about it freshman year, though the details about what happened there were kept entirely secret.

"It's the third day when it happens—Sunday," seniors would say, smiling knowingly at one another. "And I guess that's fitting because we all know who else had a big third day. JESUS. When he rose? But really: Nothing can prepare you for Kairos's third day."

When I finally had the chance to go, I did experience it as an intoxicating weekend. Away from our cliques and extracurriculars, we sat cross-legged in a circle, cued up a Jewel CD, and poured out our pain.

"I feel gross and different!" we all bellowed.

"Me too! I had no idea!" we all replied.

On our third day, we got letters from students who had gone on the trip before. That was the huge reveal—prior attendees had written personalized letters of encouragement for us to read, full of compliments and advice. "You are brave enough to speak in class. Perhaps you should try a career that involves public speaking, like the person who makes the lost kid announcements at the grocery store!"

The weekend worked on me, just like so many things about prayer and Mass and the sacraments worked on me. It all made me feel connected and significant. Anyway, retreat lyfe. Solidarity trips. I found that again at BC, where it was hip to be a faith-based activist. We even had a term for it: "social justice-y."

Us social justice-y kids ran the campus, leading roving prayer circles and organizing talks about social inequity in South and Central America. We moved like a tide of held-together-by-safety-pins JanSport backpacks, attending class during the day, lecture series at night, and Mass on the weekend.

I declared Theology as my major and added a minor in Faith, Peace & Justice, which I thought would make me more marketable. What business doesn't care about justice? With academic, Catholic, and social justice boxes checked, the last thing I needed to complete my identity quadfecta was athletics—so I promptly joined the rugby team.

BC was a Division 1 sports school, so I wasn't recruited to play sports there; apparently their ideal athlete wasn't the slow lane swimmer who hid in the showers during practice. The two club sport options were crew and rugby. The crew team had to get up at four a.m. and run to the boathouse for practice. The rugby team could wake up a little bit later. This was the bulk of the information I weighed.

The deciding factor for me was Nate, who I was still dating long-distance. Having spent so much time at his football games and sometimes even training with him, I understood and liked football. Since we'd gotten to school, we'd stopped clicking in some fundamental way—probably because I am a lesbian—and I thought that my playing a similar sport to his would help us to communicate better. Is that what straightness feels like? You play similar sports?

Rugby was a blast. We sáng songs taught to us by our genuine-Irish-like-from-Ireland coach and hit each other hard and threw each other over our shoulders, which is part of rugby, and we drank out of shoes, which is also part of rugby. We were also bad. If I had to describe the typical BC woman, she'd be white and blond and wearing a hoodie to go eat a chicken stir-fry sub sandwich with cheese, an actual food everyone fucking loved to eat on campus. We constantly played Smith, one of the top teams in the league, and we'd be out on the pitch all tiny and spiritual and stir-fried and they would crush us with their thighs that clearly did leg presses and their ambiguous faith expressions. Man. Smith. I'll tell ya. Those gals had short hair on their heads and long hair on their legs and I had truly never seen adult(ish) women like that before. A whole team of Lea DeLarias, ready to tackle me. Yum!

This is where I should probably mention that the entire time I was there, Boston College's nondiscrimination policy did not include sexual orientation. Though I never saw it happen, the university's stance at the time was that it should have the right to remove students and faculty from the school if they were found out to be gay. Sexual orientation wouldn't be incorporated as a protected class until after I graduated, in 2005. This wasn't something they just hadn't updated; it was a specific and intentional omission that reflected—and informed—years of real discrimination on campus.

Here's something I didn't know until I was writing this book: My freshman year, the *Princeton Review* ranked BC second of 345 colleges in the "alternative lifestyle not an alternative" category—in other words, it was the second most homophobic college in the country.[1] Number one went to Notre Dame. It's probably safe to say that BC wasn't in the top two choices for out queer folks applying to college.

Nonetheless, I was having a grand old time between rugby, classes, and carrying the message of Cool Jesus when, in the middle of my sophomore year, the *Boston Globe* published the results of its initial investigation into the sexual abuse scandal in the Catholic archdiocese of Boston. Maybe you saw *Spotlight*. The stuff in that movie is what I'm talking about.

If you didn't see it, in 2002 the *Boston Globe* broke the story that Bernard Law, then the archbishop of Boston, had been hiding sexual abuse by priests within the archdiocese. It was sinister, criminal, human-garbage behavior—priests he knew to be rapists weren't turned over to the police, prosecuted, removed from their positions of power. Instead, they were relocated to other churches, where they harmed entirely new sets of kids. This wasn't the first time the Church had to answer for pedophile priests, but it was a singularly awful moment. The team at the *Globe* wrote more than six hundred articles about the abuse, giving detailed information about scope and intention that forced Law to resign as archbishop. For context, the archbishop is the leader of the Church in Boston, and BC is the largest Catholic college in the city. He was technically the boss of our school. And he was far from the only person damned by the truth that year. In a matter of months, five priests were arrested. Similar news broke in other cities. All of this unspooled on the front page of the newspaper I read walking across campus where I was a Theology major and where definitely no gay people existed or could come out.

It broke my heart, seeing the Church the way it really is. As an abuser. As darkness. As a bulldozer that decimates and has decimated communities, cultures, and countries for the duration of its existence. Yes, Catholics can do good in the world. There are priests and nuns and schools and groups of people doing solid work for the poor or the sick who belong to that faith. I was trying to be one of those people. Until I wasn't.

Around the same time as the Spotlight team published their first stories, I went to a debate hosted by the Theology Department about whether women should be allowed to enter the priesthood. That's what was being discussed on campus. Not how the fuck we could belong to an organization run by abusers and people who were complicit in abuse. The debate was held in Gasson Hall, the campus building pictured on all the brochures, and it felt very official.

I walked in late and caught some dude I knew lecturing on the deficit women face against God's true image. Women are vessels taken from Adam's rib. Women should obey as Mary did. Women will be given tasks by the Lord and must fulfill them. Women cannot stand on an altar and take up space and consecrate Mass and interpret the Bible and write theory and create law. Everything he said, this nineteen-year-old boy I sat next to in class, was something I, too, had thought about myself. Something I'd been taught. But that day, as I heard him speak it so arrogantly, so definitively, while the men who ran the Church in our city had been exposed as pieces of shit who had nothing to do with holiness, I changed. In fact, my jaw unhinged and I ate him. As I digested him, I remember thinking, *Well, shit, I think my Catholicism broke.*

Truly, that was it for me.

I started to think about church elders who had access to a whole lot more life experience and information than this young guy in Gasson Hall and *still* bought into this system. I wanted to ask them, "Are you telling me you're eighty years old and you don't think women are equal to men on the most basic level? Or is it just that you love living in this gorgeous stained-glass house?"

The independence and autonomy of living away from home allowed me to see the bigger picture for the first time. I began to look back at my own history and see that this bullshit had been with me all the while. Like at Benet, when a friend of mine asked me to run for student council with him. He'd be vice president; I'd be president. I told him I didn't think a woman could ever be student council president. I just didn't think students would vote for a chick. Looking around, the school had a male president, male principal, male vice principal, male dean, and a bunch of priests and monks. There was one female assistant dean and one nun. I ran instead for vice president, alongside a different guy friend. We lost to the dude who had asked me to be the president on his ticket.

That still irks me and so I would like to promise you, reader of this book, that if I am elected student council president I will rig all the vending machines in your office to disperse free snacks between noon and two every Friday!

Once I'd realized women were not simply empty wombs, other dominoes began to fall. If saying "all women can't do something" was reductive, for example, how could I feel that abortion was definitely evil? I wanted to call up the Pope and say, "I'm young, and I'm pretty sure I'm not a genius, but this makes no sense and

I can't be smarter than all you priests by this much." Either the Church's prescriptive views were being defined and presented by people who knew they were a lie, or they *didn't know* they were lying—and I couldn't figure out which was more terrifying. I felt like I was on the other side of some wide chasm, looking back and wondering, *What is everyone doing back there?*

Still, I tried to hang in, hoping my faith might return. During my junior year, I studied abroad in Rome, where I went to an audience with the Pope. There were thousands and thousands of people crowded into a giant auditorium, chanting things like "JP2, we love you!" Then, instead of John Paul II, who was in his early eighties at the time, walking out onto a balcony, *a balcony was rolled out with him already on it*. The atmosphere was 100 percent Céline Dion concert. Second Céline reference *IN THIS CHAPTER*! I'm thinking of getting a print of Céline in her wedding dress framed for my home.

I am in the first generation of Catholics to really experience the Church's image transition from above the people to *of the people*. During my childhood, Mother Teresa was famous *and* a nun, which was a new thing. There she sat, on the cover of *Time*, holding the sick and the poor. John Paul II, the second-longest-serving Pope in several lifetimes, had been Pope my whole life. All modern Popes before him had been Italian, and he was Polish, which made him seen as more a "man of the world." He smiled often (radical!), traveled the world (progressive!), started studying for the priesthood during World War II, and was anti-Communism during the Cold War. I'd seen him give Mass before, even seen him making someone a saint during a canonization, but I'd never seen this: At the audience, he knelt on his octogenarian knees for hours and spoke five different languages. I was really impressed. He was like a grandfather shared by millions.

An evil grandfather, though, despite his smiley, liberal demeanor. For instance, John Paul II was a "no condoms, ever" kind of guy. His hard stance against contraception had a direct effect on the AIDS crisis in Africa, where many relief organizations are faith-based. Doctors and AIDS activists have pointed to the lack of condoms—and specifically the Pope's role in that—as the main cause for the spread of HIV there, which led to an epidemic of deaths.

See? Evil.

But he didn't look evil! He had a cute little face and a Popemobile and also owned a big stockpile of land. Did you know that? The Pope owns the third most land in the world, behind the Queen of England and the King of Saudi Arabia, and the Church itself is one of the world's wealthiest organizations in land and liquid wealth. It also owns LOTS of priceless art and doesn't pay tax or report income. And it does a lot to protect its wealth. Like consider this: The reason priests can't get married is because back in the day, if they had kids—well, if they had sons—those sons would have been able to inherit Church land.

It's fucked up to teach children that the Bible is fact-based and literal. That penance is required for thoughts or tiny mistakes. I'll never truly lose the dread and fear that any choice I make or even the way I simply am will lead to consequences and pain for myself and others that are eternal.

For example, just the other day I didn't tip a salesperson on the iPad thing that you pay on now and I thought about it for days, berating myself. *They probably didn't get paid a fair wage to scan that bottle of iced tea and what did I do? I dropped the ball on leaving them extra. I signed with my finger and left. And now it's my fault that their small son Tim will have a very tiny turkey this Christmas before dying an early death.*

Fuck!

So maybe it was less like I grew up with an angelic grandpa and more like I grew up with a very rich, very shitty dad who told me I was born broken and that my only shot at being okay was membership in a family where women are inherently less than?

Just like Donald Trump Jr.!

And John Paul II wasn't some outlier. The next Pope, Benedict XVI, had been Pope John Paul II's protégé when he went by his pre-Pope name, Cardinal Joseph Ratzinger, which sounds like the name of a villainous cartoon rat. In 1986, as cardinal, he published a particularly damning letter titled "Pastoral Care of Homosexual Persons" in which he called homosexuality a "strong tendency ordered toward an intrinsic moral evil," and an "objective disorder."[2]

So when the current Pope is retweeted into my feed for saying something moderately progressive about climate change, I do get a bit annoyed. The Church hasn't reversed its stance on contraception, abortion, women, homosexuality, colonialism, or moved to actually love and support people in constructive and life-saving ways *as we are.* This green hippie recycling peace-and-love Pope still heads up a faith that shelters sexual predators. Unfollow, block.

Which brings me back to BC and 2002. There was something else cooking on campus that particular year. The fact that sexual orientation wasn't covered by the school's nondiscrimination policy had worked its way into the collective consciousness. I wish I knew exactly how—who decided that the school was lagging on its protection of some of its most vulnerable students. I do know that signs started appearing in dorm room windows and op-eds in the school paper asking the administration to change its policy. Some faculty started displaying "Safe Zone" posters in their classrooms because they were adults who lived in the world and understood that many of their students, percentage-wise, had to be queer. Perhaps it would seem that this indicated a safer campus overall, but that's not how it felt to me. It felt like these small shifts revealed greater obstinacy and opposition. Some classes were "Safe Zones," but those made the other classes implicitly unsafe zones, and there were more of those. There was no question how the overall campus felt about queer folks.

Cultural shifts are like that—they can bring the horrors of the status quo into greater relief.

So, during the spring of my sophomore year, right after the Spotlight papers had been published and I'd watched the debate about women priests, as students and faculty at BC began the first push to provide a safe and open campus for queer students, I went on a solidarity trip to Jamaica.

My classmates and I spent the majority of the trip in inner-city Kingston. The last three days of the mission trip, we did a silent retreat on Church-owned beachfront property in Montego Bay. Montego Bay is essentially an assortment of Señor Frog's restaurants and white people getting their hair braided. The thing is, even though Jamaica is an island, many Jamaicans can't swim because the coastal areas were stolen by colonizers or bought up by non-Jamaican companies. My group of students had read all about the ways Jamaicans were separated from the wealth of their land, and then there we were, sunbathing on it amid some crucifixes.

This didn't even seem that strange to me. Priests who are part of an order follow the views of a specific saint and live in community. They also often take a vow of poverty. But priests can also work for a church, a school, an archdiocese, or the Vatican and live in regular layperson housing without taking a vow of poverty. I knew priests who lived in fancy condos and drove Audis.

Nuns, on the other hand, can only be part of an order. They *must* take a vow of poverty. Oh well! Women don't like Audis.

During this trip to Jamaica, we visited a hospice and I met a woman who was blind. She was sitting alone, eating a banana. We couldn't communicate; she spoke Jamaican Creole. So I sat with her for a while and after a few minutes, she reached for my hand and started saying the Hail Mary in English. I joined her and we said it together, over and over. Religion is complicated. As soon as you've listed every reason it's the worst, you find someone who wants to pray and there you are, praying.

While in Jamaica, we went to a leper colony, a home for abandoned children, and a school. Probably nothing I did during that time had a lasting effect on the lives of the people I met, but the trip had a lasting effect on me: One of the social justice-y BC kids I traveled there with became my first girlfriend.

GETTING GAY

Her name was Jo. She was a long-distance runner. I didn't know it at the time, but she was just my type: tangled, kind, layered. Generally, she gave a shit. She was close with her family and had just lost her father to cancer the summer before. She was sad and thoughtful and open and tough. Growing up with as much Jesus as I did, I tended to approach relationships with a real Bob the Builder attitude. I was a fixer, drawn to complexity and vulnerability. Today, I prefer when women tell me to fucking stop it already and that they're fine and hey focus on yourself. And I try to say it to myself, too. At the time, I just thought: *This is my new best friend.*

But that's not why I fell for her.

Jo was unlike anyone I'd met. She was from New York, where I'd never been, and she was really into emo at a time when the emotionally rocking-est thing one could do was be into emotional rock. She wore giant hot-pink rave pants but didn't attend raves and had the longest, thickest black hair I'd ever seen. When she spoke, I caught flashes of her red, white, and blue tongue piercing. "People think it's the Pepsi symbol," she said. "But that's dumb. I'd never wear a corporate symbol in my mouth, and if I did, I'd go with Coke, which tastes way better."

We started talking on the flight over and didn't stop for ten days. Well, that's not totally true. During our trip's three-day silent retreat we didn't talk. There, we simply felt each other's breath and touched each other's hair. She was the first person I'd really connected with who shared my passion for change and action. For her, it wasn't religious—she didn't love God and Mary and Jesus and everyone in the sky sooooo much—but the approach was the same. We took early-morning walks and saved a place for one another at every meal and I loved her.

One of the places we visited was a home for kids born HIV positive. The Jamaican medical system hadn't given their families support, so the parents left their kids at this home run by nuns to receive medical attention. Many of the kids had physical disabilities and didn't have the necessary adaptive equipment like wheelchairs, crutches, leg braces, etc. The place was understaffed, with minimal resources, and the programming was bare bones life and death stuff.

We were there to provide a day's worth of individualized attention and generally assist in any way we could. When we walked in the room, we saw that the children were in cribs, no matter their age, and extremely thin. I went over to a young girl, maybe six years old, who had cerebral palsy. She was on her belly and I put my hand on her arm and she smiled. When I picked her up, I realized that her body had been shaped to the crib. She had been on her belly for so long that her arms, head, and neck all tilted as if she were permanently lying in that position.

Holding her, I started to tear up. I didn't mean to, and I definitely didn't want this young girl to feel pitied. A second later, Jo appeared and sat down next to me, holding a different child in her arms. She didn't say anything in particular to me, or maybe at all. I can't remember. She was just there—and I knew I wasn't going to change this kid's life. But the choice in that moment was between her being in a crib or being held, and human connection seemed preferential. Still, this short-term attention felt basically useless, and I saw the same feeling in Jo's eyes when we looked at each other.

Our last few days in Kingston were spent at a school. It had been built in a neighborhood that was later annexed by the city dump. As the trash mounded, the landfill spread beyond its initial confines and pushed its way between houses and businesses. Eventually, it pushed its way under the school. The teachers stayed. The students stayed. The landfill and the school became one place. We read with the students, played soccer, and then hopped in a bus and a nun drove us to Montego Bay for the retreat. As we rattled through the rain forest, I laid my head in Jo's lap. *What an intimate and completely heterosexual new best friendship I have struck up with this young woman*, I thought, looking up at her.

The day we returned to campus, I had plans to catch up with my boyfriends.

I was dating two men at the time. One was the terminally chill Joshua. Raised by two feminist teachers at an all-boys school in rural New England, Joshua knew how to talk to women, how to mountain bike through rough terrain, and mostly, how to relax. He had the biggest hookah on campus. Kids would gather in his room and grab one of the dozen hoses from his pipe while he lit up the strawberry tobacco using a piece of flint. Joshua had tousled shoulder-length hair and a full beard, and he wore a white robe and rope belt to parties. Facially, he looked a lot like Elvis, and stylistically, a lot like Jesus. He looked like Elvis/Jesus, the King of Kings. He had a soothing, deep voice and a gentle manner, and I would have been friends with him if I knew that being just friends with a guy was possible.

And then there was Ian. We'd met within a few days of arriving at BC. He was from the Midwest, too—not Chicago, but we had a connection nonetheless. He lived in the next dorm over from mine freshman year, and we began to run in similar circles of friends. He was a huge man, thin but with broad, overdeveloped shoulders and massive hands and feet that gave him a build reminiscent of a pro swimmer. He had a Bic'd head, a booming voice, and he never stopped moving and he never stopped talking. He didn't do drugs, but he had the wild-eyed intensity of a Wall Street banker whose coke bump has just taken effect. It was as if his body was a cocaine factory. Almost immediately after we met, Ian began this habit of picking me up—like off the ground—and carrying me around. He was more than a foot taller than me. When he'd pick me up, I actually couldn't get myself down until he decided to put me down. He was charismatic and intimidating.

When I'd first arrived at BC, having Nate as a boyfriend was a perfect situation. Cell phones and email weren't really things yet, our schedules didn't line up, we only talked every couple of days, and we didn't really see one another. I had photos of him to hang in my room, stories about him to tell to my new friends, and a reason to not be dating anyone at BC. I was just another unaware gay saved from straight sex by long-distance love.

Most importantly, my relationship prevented any expectation that I might go on dates or make out with dudes at parties. Midway through freshman year, though, some weeks after I'd gone to visit him in DC, Nate and I broke up. I ended it with him, asking for a "break" when I meant a "breakup." I was unable to articulate any reason. Two weeks later, when he called to check in on the "break," I told him I'd canceled my trip to visit him during spring semester. I just let us fade away. I was brokenhearted to lose Nate as a support system, but also felt free. No more touching! No more snuggling! No more hand jobs while watching *Speed 2* in theaters!

That freedom didn't last for long. As soon as things ended with Nate, Ian began asking me to hang out on weekends. I'm not sure how he knew I was recently single, except that Ian knew everything about me all the time. Perhaps he asked around? Or maybe he tapped my phone line? (Idk: This dude was scary.) Because we were in vaguely the same circle of friends, at some point he had figured out a way to track down my schedule. He seemed to always know where I was—what class, what party, what dorm room. He would come there and find me. And when he wasn't picking me up, he'd knock me down. He'd wait behind a tree or around a corner and then sneak up and tackle me to the ground. It was embarrassing and I didn't want to draw more attention to myself, so I'd half play-fight back, half really fight back. Either way, it was useless. I always had to wait until he was ready to let me go.

As much as I'd enjoyed being out of the mix during my relationship with Nate, it was hard watching my friends date. Moaning about their crushes was one of my friends' favorite pastimes. But there were no boys I had crushes on. Ian was someone I could talk about with them. He was the easiest answer to the question, "Who are you into, Cameron?" I thought attraction was a decision and, just like with Bass Boy when I was fifteen, I decided to be into the guy who was into me.

I was casually dating both Ian and Joshua when I left for that trip to Jamaica. Personality-wise, I was attracted to both of them. Physically, I found it extremely easy to not have sex before marriage with either of them.

I was invited to two parties the night Jo and I came back from Jamaica: one thrown by Ian and one by Joshua. The next day I was scheduled to fly back to Chicago for my little sister's confirmation ceremony. With nothing ahead of me but an afternoon flight the following day, I invited Jo to go party-hopping with me. She'd heard a lot about the two men I was dating and I figured she'd definitely want to meet them.

Jo arrived at my dorm, which smelled overwhelmingly tropical. I had side-eyed the white people with braids in Jamaica only to return home and attempt to Bob-Marley-dread my hair using coconut oil, which definitely isn't how you do that. Also: Don't, Cammy, NO! Jo said something noncommittal about my new look and then we left for the parties.

First stop: Ian. He and his brother—a senior!—were throwing a Jell-O-shot-fueled rager. We stayed for an hour or so, monitoring keg stands and chatting with Ian's brother's exotic twenty-one-year-old friends before I kissed Ian goodbye. Across campus, Joshua was having pals to his dorm room to watch *The Matrix* and smoke green-apple-flavored shisha. We watched part of the film there before bailing due to general lethargy—red wine does not improve upon allegorical storytelling. Joshua asked me to stay the night, but I shooed him aside with a kiss. "Enjoy the rest of the movie," I said. "We're leaving. I need Jo to walk me home." I lived just down the hall.

I still remember how slowly I punched in the key code on my dorm room door—I took my time in willing none of my seven suitemates to be home. And they weren't. We had the place to ourselves. Jo walked me into the central living area and over toward the couch. She leaned against its back, perched on the edge, and said something like "It's strange to be back."

As I looked at her in that moment, a Rolodex flew open in my mind. I shuffled through each night I'd left Joshua's dorm room to hurry back to my own. I saw myself run from a party to avoid going home with Ian. It was like a director's commentary was suddenly playing over my entire life. I reached for Jo, stopping just before my hand touched her cheek, and whispered, "Could I kiss you?"

"Yes," she said, and I put my palm against the left side of her face and leaned in.

It was a big reveal, this kiss. It was Bruce Willis realizing *he* was dead and the guy from *Memento* reading his tattoos and Joaquin Phoenix swinging away all rolled into one. It was pure clarity, an instant solution to my tiny gay Rubik's Cube of a life. Everything lined up. This was my first real sexual experience. I was twenty years old.

Jo and I were interrupted about thirty seconds later by the arrival of one of my suitemates. I sprang away from our kiss with such fervor that I pushed Jo backward over the couch and then immediately relocated to the other side of the room to make it seem like we were just regular gal pals who hang out while one person is upside down on a couch with her feet in the air and the other is ten feet away yelling, "Well, anyway!" Jo left not long after.

When I woke up the next morning, I felt equal parts panicked and elated. Panicked because I really didn't want to go to hell, and elated because I had just figured out how my body worked. What's more, I felt a greater capacity for romantic love than I had ever imagined. I wanted to call Jo immediately and propose, though since same-sex marriage was illegal nationwide at the time, exactly what I would propose wasn't clear. I just knew I felt desperate to see her again. Oh, and I felt itchy. On my face.

What I didn't know at the time was that I had contracted facial ringworm during the trip to Jamaica, probably at the school on the landfill. Ringworm is a fungus that causes a perfect circle of raised red bumps to form on the skin. I had it on my cheek, and even though I felt bumps with my hand, nothing could have prepared me for my glance in the mirror that morning.

Let's say you want to fuck with a very Catholic kid. First, make sure she's seen *The Exorcist*—perhaps has even recently experienced the actual *Exorcist* staircase—and is casually aware of the characteristics of demonic possession, e.g., pea soup vomit and the sprouting of red bumps that spell words. Then, the morning after she has kissed a woman for the first time, have her wake up with a bunch of screaming red bumps right on her face. Have them form the letter O, probably for "ovaries." It was a real *The Scarlet Lesbian*–type situation.

I arrived home in Chicago later that afternoon with one hand on my cheek, but I couldn't cover the O for long—my mom noticed it the moment she saw me. Luckily, ringworm is easily treatable. My parents called the doctor and I had a prescription for a fungus-fighting cream within a few hours.

Ringworm is also very contagious, especially before it is treated. And it just so happened that I had kissed three different people the night before it appeared. So, while I wanted to call Jo and say, "Hi, Jo. You are perfect and amazing and the reason for my existence. And I love your hair," I ended up asking, "How itchy would you say your face is?" And then called Ian and Joshua, asking them the same question, desperately hoping none of them would get it. That could have made for some awkward conversations in the dining hall.

As it was, none of them caught ringworm. I eventually did tell Jo those sweet things and we dated for three years. But first, within hours of selling my soul to Satan, I had to show up for Britton's confirmation, since I was her sponsor.

Confirmation is the sacrament when you become an adult in the Church. A bishop performs the ceremony. And usually confirmandi (that's the word for it!) choose a full adult as their confirmation sponsor. Lotta aunts get the job. A few uncles. Britton had chosen me. And I took it as a huge compliment, because sponsorship is supposed to be a lifetime commitment. You become that person's primary spiritual guide.

Britton wrote me a letter before her confirmation. I still have it. *I am so proud that you will be serving as my sponsor,* she wrote. *I was once told that when you go to Heaven, the clothes you wear are your good deeds. If you don't do a lot of good to the world, your clothes will be very scrawny and unattractive. If you do a lot of good, you will have a beautiful patchwork gown of your good deeds. You, Cameron, would have the most beautiful long, graceful, silky gown. You will be the most trendy person there. I love you so much, and I honor everything you do.* Then she drew a picture of Jesus on the cross with the sun shining and smiley-faced flowers all around because Catholicism can make you forget that's a dead guy.

I had always considered it really important to be a good big sister—to be someone Britton liked, admired, and respected. Especially once I went to college, which was right around the time she was starting middle school, I would go out of my way to stay engaged with her, absorbing the books, movies, and music she liked, which meant I read *A Walk to Remember* by Nicholas Sparks, watched the Mandy Moore film *A Walk to Remember*, and listened to the *A Walk to Remember* soundtrack. She really loved that property. And I loved her.

Standing with Britton during her confirmation ceremony, I wanted to barf. I was a fraud. I'd let her down and she didn't even know it. Britton knelt before the bishop and I laid my hand on her shoulder and said her confirmation name. Next, the bishop anointed her, saying "Be sealed with the Gifts of the Holy Spirit."

"Amen," she responded.

Then Britton was up on her feet, all grown in the Holy Spirit and smiling at my parents as they beamed back at her. I stood there on the altar in the church I'd been raised in and I could still feel Britton's little shoulder like an echo in the palm of my hand.

After Britton's confirmation, I flew back to Boston to finish sophomore year. I told one person what had happened with Jo: my best friend, Lindsay. We'd been friends since the minute she arrived on campus freshman year. I'd been walking across the quad carrying some "Hang in There" kitten–type poster. She was standing outside her dorm with five suitcases and a confused look on her face. "Any idea how to get inside?" she'd asked.

While I'm from the land of sausage and doughy sports fans, Lindsay is from Southern California and looked the part: short shorts and blonde hair that hung to her mid-back. This was September in Boston; no one else appeared to have stepped off a No Doubt album cover. Later I would find out that she taught surfing for an evangelical Christian church that tried to bring young beach kids to Jesus. But even without knowing that yet, I looked at her and thought, *I bet she teaches surfing for Jesus.*

I had no idea how to get her inside that dorm—mine was across campus with an entirely different registration system—but I immediately devoted myself to helping her figure it out. We became fast friends that year. I'd sleep at her place more often than I'd sleep at mine, even though I lived alone—and naturally, we decided to live in the same suite as sophomores.

I told Lindsay about Jo maybe a week after the kiss, while we sat in my car in a parking lot near the cafeteria. The thought that I might be kicked out of school and removed from my friends and studies weighed heavily on me. Even worse: I knew I wanted to kiss Jo again. I hoped Lindsay might help me come up with a plan, or at the very least allow me to gush to someone about my first love.

The engine idled. "I think I'm in love with Jo," I said.

"Like in what way?" Lindsay asked.

"Like we kissed and I would like to kiss her again," I said.

"I have to go," Lindsay said, and she got out of the car and left. I sat there for a while, trying to decide where to go or what to do next. The next time we talked, Lindsay was adamant. She hadn't spent all that time surfing for Jesus just to go soft on her best friend.

"You will go to hell for this," she said.

Lindsay didn't speak to me again for the rest of the semester. She did write me a pleading letter. *You are bigger than this*, she said. *Please, please try to fight it.* So I didn't tell anyone else.

Here's the thing. We know that being raised in bigotry—which, for now, we all are—is usually pretty injurious for us lgbtq+ folks. But we don't talk about how homophobia and transphobia affect the straight, cis friends and family who go to school with us, live with us, are friends with us, love us. I don't fault Lindsay. We both grew up breathing the same poisonous air.

This fracture in our friendship didn't last forever. Today, we are again close friends. We were both able to metabolize the poison—and I know that process affected her as it did me.

The rest of sophomore year, Jo and I met up regularly in a bizarre room in her dorm that housed only a single piano. We'd make out until I'd stop her, sobbing, and we'd go our separate ways. I'd promise myself it would never happen again, then make plans to see her tomorrow.

COMING OUT

For some reason (my parents), I landed a marketing internship at a major construction company in Chicago's Loop the summer after sophomore year, and I would like to apologize to that company for running up their long-distance bill because I spent every lunch hour hiding in a supply closet talking to Jo. Please consider it a donation to the lgbtq+ community at large.

Jo was living in Idyllwild, a California mountain town. Early in the summer, sometime in June, I received a shoebox in the mail. Opening it, I found Jo had sent a care package that included a mix CD, a hand-carved wooden monkey with extremely silly arms picked up from a roadside art dealer, a mug with the two of us hand-painted on it standing side by side, and a long, long letter. She'd sprayed the whole thing with her signature scent (Gucci Rush). This began a tradition wherein Jo would give me the most detailed, thoughtful, and communicative crafts, objects, and handwritten missives, and I would respond in kind by being like, "Have you heard this certain ABBA song? Maybe go download it for yourself using Napster."

After disastrously confiding in Lindsay, the stress of my secret was killing me. I'd stay up all night and walk around like a zombie during the day, but one of the oddly animated, uncanny-valley ones from *World War* Z. Not even a good *The Walking Dead* one.

(I've never seen *The Walking Dead*. Too scary, for god's sake. Why would I watch that? I *have* looked up photos of that character who carries the crossbow. Very much in my wheelhouse.) I was tired, but also spent that summer AMPED because I'd ACTUALLY KISSED an ACTUAL WOMAN a FEW TIMES and had trouble making eye contact with my family. I'd have torn the clothes from my body and run screaming through the streets, but I'm not much of a runner. I am historically a pretty chill person who's also good at keeping their cool, so when I saw the package on my parents' front stoop with an Idyllwild return address, I Rafiki-ed it right into the air like it was a baby Simba, proclaiming, "This is NOTHING I care about from NO ONE I've kissed!!!" or similar, and somehow from that my mom deduced something new was up in my life. It was because of that she finally made detective after all those years on the force (my mom is not a cop).

I came out to my mom that afternoon at Cafe Nordstrom. (Nordstrom: Could I please get some free stuff for saying that? I'll take three Topman suits, please. They'll need to be drastically altered to fit my cup size, which is one hundred cups, but your expert tailors can do that.) We were eating tuna fish sandwiches when I came out, a detail even I cannot believe. A more Lorelai/Rory Gilmore–esque mother-daughter team would certainly have wrangled a tuna-themed joke into the coming-out conversation. Something like:

Rory: "Speaking of tuna . . . I'm gay!"

Lorelai: "Speaking of tuna . . . okay! Now we'll have a diversity angle for your Harvard application."

Rory: "You mean a diversity angle more compelling than my being a white person from Connecticut?"

END SCENE, cue Carole King, created by Amy Sherman-Palladino.

As it was, zero vaginal fish jokes were made, which sucks. I grew up loving fish. And vagina has gotten me through years of vegetarianism. But on Coming Out Day, there were no jokes made. Very few statements, even. The entire conversation hinged on a single, unanswered question.

This is an exact transcript of how I came out:

Mom: "...Are you and Jo dating?"

Me: (stares at tuna sandwich and bursts into tears)

That ellipsis indicates a pause so pregnant, it had to be induced and then given a C-section.

Later that night, after my dad came home from work, my parents came into my bedroom and sat me down. My mom's response was mostly discomfort. My dad's was anger.

I'd been praised and validated for "holy" or achievement-related behavior my whole life.

"Cameron, you're so smart. Smarter than us."

"We love that you play with heart. You're a leader!"

"You always do the right thing."

Coming out was my first experience with letting them down. And I *really* let them down.

Parents of lgbtq+ kids: I get that your kid might feel different to you when they come out. It might feel like a new identity and it might be scary. You may feel let down and you may have to mourn the person you thought your kid was. Likely, they are sharing some of that fear and surprise. They might even mourn their other self, too. But there is so much joy in coming out. I don't mean that it always goes well, or provides safety and freedom. I am speaking only about feelings here. Feelings-wise, coming out is elating. It's a celebration.

I didn't celebrate that summer. The thing I heard most often from my parents was "We're worried about you. How will you ever get a job? Be happy? Make friends? THIS WILL KILL YOU. I mean, literally. We're worried you'll get AIDS and die."

My parents hadn't had sex ed, either, and they had no information in their church or community about gay folks. They didn't know that my sisters were statistically at higher risk of contracting HIV than I was, or that there are treatment options for HIV and AIDS. Also, they tended to worry that my sisters and I had the power to crush our futures with small acts. Like one time for an April Fool's Day prank, Allyson called my dad and said she'd pierced her nose. He cried, "How will you ever get a job? Be happy? Make friends? THIS WILL KILL YOU."

Catholicism convinced my folks that their kids were one decision away from hell at any time, and whether that was wearing a nose ring or being honest about identity, their job was to redirect, not accept. Exhausting! For them and for us.

'Cause it's not like I thought God was into nose rings and homosexuality. No, at twenty, I was like, "My best years are behind me. Guess I'll eat this whole pan of low-fat brownies and stay up all night watching reruns of *Night Court* and, if that doesn't fix things, force myself to continue dating men."

Besides being concerned about my damnation, my folks were also flummoxed by the idea that I might have an identity they didn't share, something beyond Italian Catholic Espositoness. Especially my dad. My dad is a good, smart man and a very available parent. He coached me in every sport growing up, which was endlessly frustrating and also pretty sweet. When I was in high school, he once walked for two miles across an open field between two highways in a suit and tie to make it from a train station to one of my swim meets. He was incredibly supportive, and maybe a little possessive.

Men are cultured to feel ownership over their female children. That's why dudes say things like "As the father of a daughter…" to start off their contribution to a conversation about basic human dignity for people who happen to be women. Men aren't taught to empathize with us, but to protect us as extensions of themselves. We are seen in relation or relief, rather than as distinct autonomous individuals. Living in a patriarchal society means fathers view daughters as an offering, as a good to trade to other men as a way of improving one's position. That's the history of marriage. I'd been very high achieving, which meant that my dad was a success with a solid prize to offer mankind—and my rejecting men was a rejection of his value. Not that he has ever spoken to me about any of this or made me feel it directly. It's in the dang water, man. It's the system.

Over the course of the next few years, when I heard the "There were no signs! You're not different than us!" refrain from my parents, especially my mom, it was meant with all the world's kindness behind it. But, like any human being on this planet, I want to be seen for who I am, and I'm fine if you acknowledge our differences.

My mom bounced back from our conversation at Cafe Nordstrom. Within a year or two she was reading Ellen's mom's book *Love, Ellen* about having a queer kid and swapping tales of parenthood with one of her best friends whose son had also come out. She started using the word "partner" very deliberately and, during the annual Western Springs Fourth of July parade, made everyone in my family stand and salute PFLAG as they marched past our collapsible camping chairs.

"On your feet! Look at these marchers. I wonder if any of their kids have a PARTNER."

My dad, however, cried for five years. "Your mother and I are having broccoli and you're gaaaaaaaay," he'd moan, before passing the phone over to my mom, who would be pissed at him for crying all over the broccoli and all over me. This wasn't easy on my parents' marriage—I heard them fight about whether to stay in the Church, whether to ask questions about my life. My homosexuality doesn't put a strain on straight marriage, but my parents' struggle to get on the same page because of religious bullshit sure did.

Sidebar: "How did your parents take it?" is an annoying question. It centers straight experience of queerness and someone else's disappointment instead of my joy. "How did you take it?" is a better question, although that also kind of sounds like sex talk, which I'm similarly fine with. The answer's even the same. How did I take it? Hard. Slow. With lots of discussion and negotiation and eventually a lot of relief.

After years of feeling different I finally had confirmation: I *am* different from a lot of people I know and almost everyone I grew up with—but I am also not the only one of my kind! A lifetime of feeling like a post-meteor dinosaur and now, overnight, I had words to describe myself, a neighborhood in every city, a parade every summer, and a queer family history.

Here's a list of other questions you can ask me during an

interview or if you wait in line to meet me after a stand-up show. You can only ask one. I am very busy.

- ▲ What was it like going to a restaurant with a woman for the first time?
- ▲ Do you remember the first time you held their hand in public?
- ▲ Does it still feel scary to kiss in public?
- ▲ Did anyone ever scream anything shitty at you while you were doing so?
- ▲ What's it like when two queer people pass one another on the street?
- ▲ And how can you identify that they're queer…what are you looking for?

When my parents came into my bedroom that June night of the Gucci Rush package, they gave me ground rules: I wasn't allowed to speak to Jo in their house or tell Britton, then thirteen, that I was dating a woman, as they worried it would be an unhealthy influence on her development. Next, the three of us went to therapy.

We weren't a therapy family. Now I love therapy. It's the best. But back then, I'd never been, and nobody in my family had ever talked about therapy, so it felt very upsetting. They sat on either side of me in what I later learned was meant to be a show of support but felt at the time like an intervention. Maybe it was their deep, deep wailing during the session that gave me that impression, or the fact that I said almost nothing while the therapist asked my parents questions. It felt like my gayness was a problem to be solved as a family, and that the therapist was there to talk me out of my sick new "lifestyle." It felt like conversion therapy lite, or at the very least, irresponsible.

When we got back home after the session, my parents suggested that perhaps I should take a year off from BC to give myself space from Jo, who was clearly a corrupting influence. They didn't want to pay for school because they thought of Boston and Jo as the source of my lesbianism. They preferred me in Chicago, where I'd been a girl who dated boys.

I was completely unprepared for this. Many people pay for their own college educations, but I had nothing in place financially that made that an option for me. As distressing as it'd been trying to reconcile my new doubts about Catholicism the previous year, not being able to return would feel even lonelier.

Meanwhile, my suitemates from sophomore year were all communicating with each other about junior year housing and apartment options. It was assumed that we would all live together again, but now I didn't even know if I'd be going back. And I couldn't exactly lay out what was going on. So I kept it vague and noncommittal—kept saying I wasn't sure what I was doing—until they found someone else to fill the spot.

By the end of my coming-out summer, I was operating like one of those nuclear tests they do in the desert: explosive, dangerous to all life forms, and best viewed from a distance while wearing a hazmat suit. Your boi Cammy was a wreck. My parents and best friend were no dice on my queerness, so I started hiding the truth from them—that I was still talking to Jo. No one fully knew what was going for me, and the future suddenly looked pretty blank, and not like in a blank-canvas-from-Michaels-you're-gonna-badly-throw-pastels-on-because-you've-decided-you're-a-painter-for-one-week kind of way. More like in the form of a giant, gaping butthole.

The loneliness remained after Allyson put two and two together and asked me whether I was dating Jo or had just started a new behavior wherein I talked about friends incessantly while describing their mouth shapes. When I said I was, she responded, "Well, I kissed a woman once in college. Didn't like it. I'm glad you do." End of discussion. She lived far away in Nashville and had never been as religious as I was, so I don't think she understood the deep level of conflict I was experiencing. I definitely couldn't talk to Britton, who apparently required protection from my bad, bad gayness.

On top of that, I wasn't super welcome in my group of high school friends since I'd broken up with Nate, not that I could imagine telling any of them what was going on, given the reactions I'd gotten thus far. Jo was in a different time zone and spending the summer in a community with a lot of out gay people and having what was, in my mind, an amazing experience of being totally out and supported.

Then, in August, Jo and her best friend drove across the country to return to school, and they routed their drive to pass through Chicago so that Jo and I could spend the night together while I lied to my parents and said I was spending the night with a male friend from college, an idea they were totally fine with (shoulder shrug emoji).

After coming up with this somehow acceptable excuse, my next mission was to figure out where Jo and I would stay. Chicago is full of beautiful hotels, and in the area where I grew up,

Marriotts abound. I had never rented a hotel room before, and needed to be back at my parents' place early in the morning to get ready for work. So I chose a locale about ten minutes from my parents' house where there are one or two motels, all with flickering signs outside that just say MOTE because the L blew out years ago and/or it's a mood, sprinkled into a landscape of approximately eighty-seven car dealerships. I didn't have a cell phone, so I told Jo the address of our *Psycho* motel, told her to print the directions off MapQuest, and said I'd meet her there at eight p.m.

I was surprised, and then suspicious, when the motel clerk asked to see my ID. Did he know what we were up to? I had no idea how renting a motel room worked. I'd gotten there first—Jo and her friend had set out probably twelve hours earlier for our eight p.m. meetup time, and this was before cell phones—so I waited in my car in the parking lot in the pouring rain with my lights on, which all felt very *Fargo*, a movie I had not yet seen.

When Jo finally arrived, I emotionally shat my pants with joy-fear but not real actual poop and then she hopped out of her friend's car and we went upstairs. The room was on the second floor and it was an enter-directly-from-outside type of place. Inside, everything was pink. Well, the walls were probably tan and the furniture probably varnished particleboard, but the single lamp was pink and the stained bedspread was pink so the room felt very pink. It was the first night we were ever totally alone together.

Very soon after we'd first kissed—it might have even been the next weekend—we had decided to go to New York City since I'd never been, had heard the salsa was good there (not like that Pace

Picante stuff), and because Jo's childhood home was only a train ride away in the Hudson River Valley. We stopped at her mom's house so we'd have somewhere to spend the night that would be less than the three million dollars it costs to simply stand in the lobby of a Manhattan hotel, breathe, and then exit.

We got upstate late at night and I met Jo's mom and sister briefly before going to bed. In the morning, her mom came to wake us up—we had an early train to Manhattan—and found us sleep-cuddling. It was briefly terrifying to be caught like this, but it ended up being okay. Not long after, Jo officially came out to her mom, who had of course deduced as much when she saw us sleeping like two little sardines with arms. Jo's mom had been very affirming, always telling Jo that she was not only good enough, but already perfect the way she was. So Jo had a check she was able to cash in with her mom. Sort of like "You always said I was great just as I am. Welp, I am gay, so that's great, right?"

By the way, we had a killer time in NYC. Jo and I arrived on ye olde island of Manhattan via Penn Station and exited directly into the staging area for a parade I'm calling That Which Does Not Kilt You, but which I believe is really entitled New York Tartan Day Parade. Anyway, it was Scottish. There were kilts and clans everywhere. Fifty different bagpiping groups were warming up simultaneously and that is actually the worst sound I've ever heard. I looked around me and thought, *Exactly what I expected; a total clusterfuck!* We pushed our way through the throng of Scots, gently grazing bare bums as we went like Russell Crowe grazes wheat and headed straight over to Rice to Riches, an entire shop dedicated to rice pudding.

Only a couple of weeks into dating her, I'd seen Jo's childhood bedroom and the city she'd visit on weekends, met her mom and sister, and been busted spooning her within view of her mom. So our night at the MOTE was a big deal: the first time Jo was near any of my world. There was no suitemate possibly arriving home at any moment. No parent watching television in the next room. There was a lock on our door and we'd paid to use it.

First, I touched her face. I'd never understood where to put my hands when kissing men. I may have held the back of Nate's head when we kissed or I might have touched Ian's arm. But when I began kissing Jo, I suddenly understood that no gesture makes more sense than resting your fingers under a person's ears, pressing your palms against their cheeks, and pulling them toward you. We were both small but she was smaller, and she had to tilt her head up to kiss me.

For a moment everything was slow. Then shit got frantic. We kissed a feral summer-apart-therapy-parents-crying kiss, Jo whipped her T-shirt off over her head as I unbuttoned her jeans and mine, and soon we were naked and lying on top of the crustiest, itchiest motel bedspread. I had seen parts of Jo—her shoulders, her breasts, and the tattoo on her left ankle—but not all of her, all together like that.

Now I ran my hands up and down her body, feeling all her unclothed skin, including the parts behind her knees. I took her nipples in my mouth. I felt her wetness on my fingers.

For the next eight hours, I felt and looked at her.

The men I had dated were muscular and slim-waisted with broad shoulders and an action figure's upside-down triangle shape. I'd compared myself against them and felt bad about myself, but Jo's body wasn't proportioned like theirs. She had strong runner's thighs and rounded shoulders. She was more petite all over than particularly small in the waist. Seeing her, I felt something new. I'd always thought my boyfriends loved me in spite of my body. I hadn't imagined that I was beautiful to them—that I turned them on. But here I was with this person and her body, which looked a lot like my body, and I was basically about to explode.

It's not like I was healed overnight, but seeing Jo that way shifted the body dysmorphia I'd been trapped within for so long, and that my heterosexual relationships were totally unequipped to bridge. It was the beginning of my understanding that you could be utterly attracted to and in love with the way a person looks without any thought of how it compares to the beauty standard that we're sold our whole lives.

Sex with a woman was new to both of us. Neither of us knew what to do, and we'd never heard about it, so we started talking about what we wanted and how we could give that to one another. It was fun, and it set an even playing field. I didn't feel pressure to keep going or to be a certain way.

With Jo, and other women after her, I felt the overwhelming chemical drive of sexuality for the first time. I found that sex is *intuitive*. That was a revelation. Not to sound too *Footloose*, but this may have been the moment I understood dancing, why it was sexy, what all the gyrating was about.

Out of nowhere I was suddenly like, *Ooooh. I get it*, and the world became one of those montages where a robot is learning very quickly by flipping through a book at super speed. My mind flashed images and theorems with statements like "Masturbation Is Great!" swirling in front of my eyes. All at once, I knew what to do.

I went down on Jo until my face was scratched raw. I reached for her and realized I was left-hand dominant during sex (left-dicked, if you will). She held me and counted the freckles on my shoulders. We "went all the way" and I lost my virginity and I didn't even feel bad about it. See, the Catholic Church made a mistake. In Catholicism, the sin of being gay is acting on it. You can be gay and celibate and that's fine with the Church. But once you break that dike, there's no distinction between kissing a girl and fisting a girl. The sin is already done. So fist away.

Well, I didn't fist *that* girl, *that* night, but we did nearly everything else and it was fantastic and emotional and orgasmless because I still had no idea how orgasm might be achieved for a vagina-haver. And I didn't feel any worse about myself than I had when we kissed.

Plus, I was disillusioned with the Church. The reporting I had read in Boston gave me reason to believe mandated celibacy was perhaps unhealthy. While this is obviously only one piece of the larger picture, it was clear that telling a human being with sexual drives to shut those down not only didn't work, but also fostered fucked-up power dynamics. I'd been taught that being celibate was holy and doable. But what I was seeing unfold in real life was that unnatural, forced celibacy affected the way some priests related to other people in horrifying ways. Plus, I'd been taught to fear premarital sex for its baby-making potential, but Jo was a cisgendered woman, so was I, there was no sperm involved, and this was all happening prior to marriage equality. What's the significance of premarital sex when you can't even get married?

No sleep happened in the pink motel room. We didn't leave the room once, not for food or anything. We didn't turn on the TV or drink any water. We had sex, repeatedly, until around six a.m., when Jo packed up and went to get her best friend wherever she had been dropped off the night before and I got in my gold Chevy Cavalier and drove home. I wondered if I would be able to return to school, if I'd ever see Jo again. I looked in the mirror in my car before walking into the house and I could see my chin and upper lip were bright red and inflamed. From Jo. I went back to my parents' house and showered and went to work like that—marked by sex—and no one even seemed to notice.

LEARNING LESBIANISM

I did go back to school the next fall. I lied to my parents and promised to break up with Jo, then left home a few weeks before school started and took buses up and down the East Coast visiting friends I wasn't out to and camping when I didn't have a place to stay. I'd bought a NASCAR sleeping bag at a fishing store on Cape Cod—one of my first stops—because I thought that would be funny, but I neglected to notice it was designated "Child-Sized" so it only went up to my waist and that felt fine, like a well-deserved punishment.

I was going to live off-campus in last-minute housing with two very sophisticated international students from Mexico City who also did some modeling on the side (look, my life has always been hard). Our apartment was several miles from BC in grungy, punk rock Allston. My new roommates were older (early twenties!), painted nude paintings of each other in the living room, and dated members of a locally famous rock band. They had a tiny orange cat named David Berkowitz who had severe intestinal problems. The whole situation felt like something Lena Dunham would have cooked up for Hannah Horvath to live in. It was the perfect place to hide. I moved in with no furniture, sheets, towels, anything—just a duffel bag, backpack, and my NASCAR sleeping skirt. I bought a squishy futon mattress on Harvard Ave., carried it home over my shoulder, and threw it in the middle of my empty bedroom to really Joanna Gaines up the place. As a finishing touch, David Berkowitz strolled by to fart on it and voilà, I was moved in.

Things got more serious with Jo. We said "I love you." I spent a lot of nights at her place and with her friends.

Joshua and I had faded away, but Ian was constantly, frighteningly, always around. I wish I could say falling in love with Jo helped me create better boundaries with Ian. It didn't. It actually made him more important to me. I still believed homosexuality was a sin. I got a spare toothbrush to leave at Jo's place, all the while imagining my place in hell. Ian was the last man standing between me and full-throttle lesbianism and I was terrified to lose him. He was who I said I was with when I disappeared to Jo's place for days without a word to my suitemates. Jo and Ian moved into the same four-unit apartment building—she lived on the first floor and he just above—which made things easy with a bit of planning and maneuvering. When I went to the apartment to see Jo, I used the back door. If I was there to see Ian, I went in the front. It was the perfect setup for a life of miserable secrecy.

This was the Drinking Hats and Goggles Era. I'm wearing rent-a-photo-booth-level accessories in the majority of pictures I have of me throughout the second half of college. Like imagine a karate gi with a hat that looks like a flamingo sitting on my head and Bono sunglasses. I have a photo of me dressed in that.

In other words, I became a master of diversion. I didn't witness anyone being expelled for being gay, but I also knew zero openly queer students among the school's more than fourteen thousand undergraduates and graduates. So I hid. Literally—at Jo's house—or figuratively, in "hilarious" costumes that propped up my party-girl mystique and protected me from accidentally wearing something too telling, like a giant rainbow flag or anything in my current wardrobe. "I'm not gay and hiding it; I'm hungover!"

I stopped going to daily Mass, playing rugby, and, for the most part, attending classes. Apart from social justice work—I still went on solidarity trips, attended pro-life protests (whoops!), and mentored younger students—the only school-related thing I was involved with was practices and shows with my college improv group, My Mother's Fleabag.

Lindsay had suggested I audition for the group at the beginning of sophomore year. Fleabag is the oldest college improv group in the country, started back in 1980 when I was negative one year old. Amy Poehler was a relatively recent alumna, and she was just starting to make it big on *SNL*, so it followed that a few years pretending to be a banana during shows in the cafeteria would lead to definite fame.

I would never have auditioned if Lindsay hadn't suggested it; being able to approach it like "this is just something someone else told me to do" took the pressure off. I went to the audition straight from rugby practice with dirt on my face, teeth, and body. I even wore my cleats.

Fleabag always has twelve members, and that particular year they were looking for three new people. I got up in front of the nine current members, did an impression of a giant squid that seemed to go over well, then headed back to my dorm, showered, and went to bed. I woke up in the middle of the night to my door being banged down and opened it to find the entire troupe standing there.

"You're in! And it's time for our secret, weird, middle-of-the-night induction ritual!"

They hauled me off into the night to an induction ritual that was quite secret and quite weird.

We practiced for six hours a week plus shows and post-practice hangouts, so I was with these eleven other people a *lot*. While there were definitely some conservative members, being a part of Fleabag felt like my first lifeline out of mainstream BC culture. The folks I'd been surrounded by at school, even my extended circle of friends, certainly drank a lot, but that was the extent of their typical college rebelliousness.

My improv group was a *tiny* bit less BC-ish. For example, one of my friends in the group smoked pot and had a Canadian girlfriend who didn't go to BC. How did he even *meet* a Canadian?! Being with folks who were slightly different from the homogeneous peer groups I'd had essentially my whole life allowed for some much-needed expansion in my worldview.

When I wasn't protesting or pretending, I was having Baby's First Queer Experiences with Jo. We would spend ninety minutes on the train to go to Diesel Cafe, a queer-owned spot out in Davis Square in Somerville that is still there and still rules. We'd go in just to use the bathroom, walk around, and *be* there. I was too scared to talk to anyone, let alone order anything. Folks there were older than us, with visibly queer hairstyles or clothing, and it all felt very intimidating. The edgiest thing someone would wear on our campus was a sweatshirt that said BOSTON COLLEGE but in a fucked-up font. I'd only seen haircuts like that when I Yahooed "lesbian." We didn't use Google yet. We didn't even have laptops. You had to flatten your desktop using an iron and then try to fold it gently and cram it into your briefcase.

When Ellen came out in 1997, I was in high school. Afterward, we weren't even allowed to speak her name in my house. I remember once watching the MTV Movie Awards when my dad walked in the back door from work at the exact moment that Selma Blair and Sarah Michelle Gellar won for Best Kiss in *Cruel Intentions*. He got furious seeing that filth on our TV, so after that, I watched *Buffy* but only the Willow parts in our basement. I was so desperate, I forced myself to sit through the scariest show that's ever been on television. This was before on-demand and TiVo and shit so I had to mute large sections of the show and unfocus my eyes so I didn't see the demons and wait for the next moment with Tara.

In college, during my sad sophomore summer, I passed my time renting movies with queer content. At the Western Springs Blockbuster, this was exclusively *Boys Don't Cry*. I think on VHS even, which was this type of brick people used to build houses before DVDs were a thing. I rewound and rewatched that movie so many times that when I returned it, it was smoking. I saw myself in Brandon, which is part of the problem with that movie because the real Brandon Teena was a trans dude and hiring cis actors to play trans characters is confusing, inaccurate, and keeps a lot of great parts away from the actors best suited to play them.

After melting *Boys Don't Cry*, I did extensive research and found *All Over Me* (what up, baby Leisha Hailey), *The Incredibly True Adventure of Two Girls in Love* (hey there, teeny Laurel Holloman), and *Paris Is Burning* (bonjour, the root of everything said on *Drag Race*), all of which I ordered to my local library, then watched standing in the basement, remote in hand, poised to turn the TV off if anyone in my family walked downstairs.

Beyond the rare overtly queer material I could find, I'd latch on to stuff that was just kinda gay if you squinted and thought really hard about it. Tegan and Sara's *So Jealous* came out after I graduated and Hayley Kiyoko wasn't even born yet (she was, and already had twelve jobs), so I had to queer up songs like "Then I Kissed Her" by the Beach Boys, which I stand by as a very gay song. I mean, "I wanted to let her know that I was more than a friend"? That's a coming-out anthem if I've ever heard one.

Jo's gay anthem was "Hands Down" by Dashboard Confessional: "Your legs are smooth / As they graze mine." SMOOTH LEGS! This song was about me and Jo! Her smooth legs grazing my smooth legs. My smooth legs grazing hers. And both of us paying shitloads of money to the razor industrial complex.

Jo got me a copy of *The Perks of Being a Wallflower*, our generation's *The Fault in Our Stars* but about teens who love The Smiths, and we read it aloud, switching back and forth each chapter. It was all very coming-of-age. Netflix had just launched as a DVD mailing service and we rented *Bound*, sent it back, and then rented it again. I am convinced that Netflix only owned one copy each of *Bound*, *Go Fish*, and *But I'm a Cheerleader* and that if we could fingerprint those copies we could create a database Home Depot would be interested in.

Jo and I hit a bunch of milestones fall semester of junior year: We showered together for the first time, watched our first gay movie in a theater (*Kissing Jessica Stein*, which I still love), managed to successfully place an actual order at Diesel Cafe, and found OUR SONG (David Gray's "This Year's Love," which is really too sad, good lord)—before parting ways to both spend spring semester studying abroad.

I went to Rome.

I was still a Theology major, after all.

Okay. Remember how my eyes are gnarly and sometimes crossed? The moment I arrived in Rome, my eye crossed all the way. It hadn't happened this badly since I was two. And along with the crossing came double vision. Because this was often triggered by exhaustion, I got some extra sleep and assumed it would correct itself when I was over my jet lag. For days I tried to make do tripping on cobblestones, walking into walls, and wearing black turtlenecks from the Gap like any other European. Then I attended the audience with the Pope. When I saw two John Paul IIs come onstage, I finally realized something was very wrong.

I called my parents from the one available phone at the Italian college where I lived. It was in a freezing-cold marble hall; you had to take calls in a very *Carol* public manner. My parents reached out to my eye doctor in Chicago, who said that the crossing was likely due to psychological stress. My parents suggested that it was the stress and strain Jo was putting on me; I wasn't gay and this was my body's way of giving me the hint.

While "your eyes are trying to bail on your gay behavior" was one explanation, the other possibility was the same that'd been true when I was a kid: brain tumor. Without doing tests, there was just no way of knowing. So to be on the safe side, my parents helped me get an appointment with a local Roman eye doctor. Actually, Italy has socialized medicine, so I literally went to see the Pope's eye doctor. His office was panic inducing, with rusty, sepia-toned instruments and heavily gauzed people, and my

Italian is awful enough that I basically walked in, yelled "Meatball!" and hoped for the best.

The Italian doctor's solution was prism glasses, which are giant metal frames with super-serious lenses that attempt to correct the crossing while giving the wearer an air of Mad-Eye Moody. When I looked in the mirror, I saw a construction site happening on my face. They weren't going to send me for a CT scan or any follow-up tests to rule out a tumor or other causes. As I've said, double vision, if left alone, can cause permanent blindness in one eye. What if this dude was wrong about the prism glasses? What if I lost my vision? What if it was something more serious? So I stumbled back through the Vatican, the most direct path from the hospital to my dorm, and back to the 1940s-era telephone. Two days later and straight from the airport, a doctor in Chicago immediately deduced that I had been overprescribed for contact lenses and would need emergency surgery to save my vision.

When you're a kid and you have eye muscle surgery, they put you to sleep, use lasers, wake you up, and then your mom or dad or aunt gives you a Popple. When you're an adult, it's way more hard-core. The doctor snips the muscles on the side of your eye and threads a loose suture into the muscles that keep your eye in its socket. Then they wake you up, and while you are fully alert, the doctor pulls on the suture like it's a set of venetian blinds until your eye is straight. Did you read what I just wrote? I was awake *while a doctor adjusted my eyeball on a string*. Do you even know anyone more badass than me?

After surgery, I remained home for two weeks to heal. Valentine's Day fell in the middle of my recovery. I was still half-bandaged and feeling crappy overall. Jo was eight hours ahead of

Chicago time, studying abroad in South Africa, it was our first Valentine's Day, and I was spending it bloody-eyed and at home with my still-reeling-from-the-gay parents, lovesick but unable to gather the courage to ask to make a long-distance call under their roof. It was a scene written by John Green.

To cheer me up, my mom suggested that we take Britton, then thirteen years old and learning Spanish in school, to see Pedro Almodóvar's *Talk to Her*, which was playing in the next town over. If you haven't seen this film, let me start by saying, it is not the best to see with your mom and teenage sis, and it's not the best for Valentine's Day. For example—SPOILER ALERT—the film features an awful, *Kill Bill*–esque coma-sexual-assault scene. It also features a twenty-foot-tall vagina.

There is a part in *Talk to Her* where an adult man shrinks down to the size of a tampon and walks into a vagina. Almodóvar isn't one for cutting-edge digital effects, so he built an enormous vagina set complete with palm tree–sized pubic hair. As the giant vagina flickered on-screen, all three of us—my mom, my sister, and I—sat there and stared. We didn't leave early. We didn't comment on what was going on. We sat and pretended that twenty feet worth of vagina wasn't in front of our faces. I was literally unable to avert my eyes, or at least one of them, having recently had it sewn into place.

This moment is a great metaphor for the coming-out process. Remember when you had to sit through a sex talk from your parents that was important and necessary but also horrifically embarrassing? (I didn't have that, but I know it's a thing.) Coming out feels like that sex talk in reverse: You sit your folks down and say things they probably find too informative and too uncomfortable. It feels confrontational and clinical. I'd like to thank Pedro Almodóvar for allowing me to take that abstract feeling and translate it into a real-life experience.

This still stands as one of my most memorable February fourteenths, perhaps only bested by the time I attended a Valentine's Day monster truck rally during which the stadium caught fire. Some pyrotechnics got pushed over by Grave Digger or whomever, and the side of the arena started to burn while whole families of monster-truck fans cheered wildly and remained in their seats, seemingly ready to die, until the monster-truck equivalent of a rodeo clown doused it.

My parents would struggle with my queerness for years. But there was something temporarily healing in going home that February in such a vulnerable state. Between the baby glasses, surgery, and many trips to the ER for my various depth-perception-related injuries, my crossed eyes gave my parents a special reason to protect me, and this surgery seemed to bring that out in them again.

Recovery was quick but excruciatingly painful. I couldn't move my eyes at all for a few days afterward, so I was generally helpless. In spite of the miserable summer we'd endured together, my parents took great care of me. It was a brief window of opportunity to relate to each other in a more familiar, loving way. There were lots of tears at the airport when they took me back to O'Hare so I could finish my semester. The first non-"our daughter's gay" tears in a long time.

I got back to Rome after missing a month of school for my surgery and somehow made up my classes. During time off, one of my friends took me on a road trip through the French countryside from Rome to Normandy in the BMW her parents had purchased for her to drive while she lived in Europe. At least that's the story she told me. Maybe she was a spy. We stopped in Florence and picked up Jo's best friend. She knew about me and Jo, but my BMW-driving friend was a very devout Catholic and didn't. On our way through the Alps, we took a turn and found that the road had been taped off. Silly vandals! We moved aside the tape and eased the BMW up the curving road only to find a few sharp twists later that the road suddenly ended because there had been an actual avalanche. There was no guardrail and the tiny local road wasn't wide enough to do a three-point turn (or honestly even a twenty-point turn). So our only option was to slowly reverse down a snowy guardrail-less road for the length of a literal Alp in a stick shift car. *Well,* this *will be a glamorous way to go,* I thought quietly to myself so as not to distract our very Catholic driver. *Except it will suck to not even have been out to one of the two people involved in my epic mountain death.*

Jo and I emailed with' the frequency of two lesbians in love before the time of WhatsApp or international text messaging and hatched a grand romantic plan. Jo's mom and sister wanted to visit her, and Jo somehow convinced her mom that they should meet in Italy. It had been a family-only trip, and Jo's mom and sister left one night before Jo had to go back to South Africa, agreeing to let us stay in the same hotel room that the three of them had shared. It was a major upgrade from the pink motel. Picture spacious and fancy, with an actual pillar in the center of the room.

Jo and I had set ourselves up for a pretty dramatic get-together. We were fighting for our love against outside forces: angry parents and friends, an intolerant school, and continental divides.

I'd had a serious surgery and one of my eyes was still completely red. Plus, we were in Rome, the holiest of cities, on Easter weekend. In keeping with the drama, our meeting spot was the Trevi Fountain.

The stakes were as high as can be. We had one night together, and we *both* had our periods? Beat that, Ethan Hawke and Julie Delpy. So we had our first period sex. And it was GREAT. I had terrible cramps and it helped, and it was intimate, beautiful, and pretty smelly, like the butcher case at a grocery store.

Having gay sex with my girlfriend while I was living in Rome, steps from the Vatican, studying Theology kind of sounds like an active fuck-you to Catholicism, but it wasn't like that. I honestly wasn't thinking too much about the Pope.

We left the hotel room looking like several bodies had been dismembered there, but not before the murder victims grabbed at every wall with their bloody, bloody hands.

Ah, Roma!

SURVIVE

A few years after college, I was sitting shotgun on a drive between Manhattan and Cape Cod, Massachusetts. My buddy Ben was driving. Mo and Claire were in the back seat. We were all young comics, out on a slapdash tour. With no booking agents to work out the details for us yet, we had conveniently booked shows in Chicago, Cleveland, Baltimore, and Provincetown, Massachusetts—you know, those neighboring cities. That's the kind of glorious routing you get with a self-planned, three-years-into-stand-up tour. If you've been in Baltimore and thought, *Let's take an eight-hour drive to the end of whatever state juts most toward England and camp outside between shows so we can test this friendship!* then you know what it is to be a stand-up comic just starting to work the road.

The four of us had detoured to Manhattan to spend the night at Ben's Lower East Side apartment because we would rather drive through the busiest city in the world than pay $34 for a hotel room between Baltimore and Ptown. We were splitting $150 per show four ways; that $34 just wasn't going to happen. We were exhausted from looking at each other and hadn't had a damn minute to shit in peace in four days. That, my friend, is when you start telling sex stories. I think Ben started it, actually. He told the story of a recent exploit—he'd met a boy while doing shows in

London, they'd hit it off so well that Ben decided to return the following month, except there was some sort of returning joke-teller visa snafu at the border and he had to fly back home without ever leaving the airport. It was a good story—would have worked as a *Love Actually* subplot—but I knew I had better.

I'm cocky about my sex stories. After college, I really kicked it into high gear to experience everything I missed between thirteen and nineteen with a sort of "race 'round the world" mentality. I underwent sage baths with yogis and had naked adventures in tree houses. By my late twenties, I'd become so stuffy—always in a relationship, always going home to spend time with my partner—that trotting out these sex stories packed an extra punch. It said, "Yo, I've done shit" and added a certain gravitas.

Usually I'd begin with my classic first smooch/facial ringworm story—but this time I decided to tell a story I'd laughed about for years with my BC suitemates. It was about a night toward the end of my sophomore year, around the time I'd first started seeing Jo, when I woke up from an alcohol-fueled blackout and didn't remember that Ian had been in my room the night before. My roommates had told me that we'd been making out with my bedroom door open, and they'd seen us fully nude and having sex. I wrapped up the story with: "So my friends told me this guy I was seeing took me home, fucked me, and left before I sobered up. I had no idea I'd even seen him the night before, and I'm not even sure if I'd *had* sex with a guy before that."

Instead of the usual laughs I'd gotten with that epic punch line, there was silence in the car. Then my friend Ben spoke up. "Cameron," he said tentatively, "it sounds like you're describing date rape."

In the years since I'd woken up that morning sophomore year with a terrible hangover and no memory of anyone else being in my room the night before, I'd never considered perhaps the evening before had been fucked up. I've since come to understand how far off my dial for healthy sexual behavior had been.

Ian *had* memorized my schedule, constantly appeared out of nowhere, and tackled and picked me up against my will. He did stalk me across campus and, without my realizing, had looked over my shoulder one day after carrying me home and memorized the numerical code to my door's keyless entry—this was to the freshman-year room that I lived in by myself. For weeks afterward, I'd come home from class and find my room had been broken into and something left inside, waiting for me. One time it was a case of beer; another time it was a pile of bricks. I only figured out it was him after I pushed the bricks in the hall and someone called campus police to have them removed. The story was printed in the police blotter in our school newspaper. Ian clipped the listing, signed it, and left it in my room.

I never knew when he might pop up, and when he did, he physically controlled when I was able to leave our interaction. I couldn't lock him out of my own dorm room. I will also say: I didn't try to lock him out. I smiled when he showed up outside my classrooms, laughed when he knocked me down as I walked across the quad, and joked with him about us making the school newspaper—but not because any of it made me happy. I thought any boundaries I set would make him uncomfortable. I prioritized his comfort over my safety.

After all, I'd been taught it was a woman's job to spurn a man's advances until after marriage, when her job shifted. She was now to provide for her husband's sexual needs and have his children. All of this was made more confusing because I didn't think I wanted to marry a man. If I wasn't going to be available to men in the way I'd been taught that women needed to be, what did I have to offer to the world? Nothing?

My relationship with Ian coincided with a new discovery: If I drank enough alcohol, I could forget where I was and forget that I wanted to leave. I could drug myself into meeting Ian's needs. To be good company to Ian, to respond to his flirting in kind, to better acquiesce, all I had to do was drink.

By the time the sophomore year blackout happened, I'd gotten used to accepting whatever he wanted from me. Of course he'd come home with me—he'd never waited to be invited anywhere I lived. Of course I felt gross for being with him—I wanted to be with Jo. Of course my suitemates didn't stop him—I'd let them think he and I were together. Of course I'd been drunk to the point of blackout—I drank to tolerate his attention and his touch.

So when my suitemates asked, "Do you remember last night? Because we saw everything," my main thought was to be embarrassed that my friends had seen me naked. I don't know if I was conscious while he was with me, or what we did that night. I do have a memory of him on top of me. I remember looking at the wall in my room. I remember him kissing me. I don't remember where we were before that. My next memory is of the morning and he's gone. If my roommates hadn't told me he was actually in my room that night, I would have perhaps thought it was a dream. I never brought it up with Ian.

Perhaps Ian's predatory presence in my life would have gone on until graduation had I not been an orientation leader the summer before my senior year. And no, not that kind of orientation. Like the kind where you show future students around and give them their EAGLES ON THE PEACE PATH shirt, or whatever their year's slogan is. The program runs continually, broken into one small group per weekend, for the length of the summer. I was one of about twenty or so upperclassmen chosen to lead these weekends—which was kind of an honor at BC—and spent the summer living on campus, working twenty-four hours a day for three days straight, and then taking four days to recover before the next group came in.

Each of the orientation leaders was required to give a speech to our coworkers before the first group of freshmen came in. The priest who ran the program instructed us to open up to one another and truly reveal our innermost selves. I decided to use the speech as a platform to come out. Sure, our boss worked directly for the university and therefore I was risking being kicked out, but I'd been to his condo in South End, which is a gayborhood, so I thought he must at least know some gay people from buying milk, or whatever priests drink. Blood? I figured this was as good a chance as I was ever going to get to start the process. I spoke for maybe four minutes total, crying through most of it, and mentioned dating a woman but without using the words *gay*, *lesbian*, or *homosexuality*. When I looked up, many of my coworkers were smiling through tears. They gave me a standing ovation. The only person who had no response was the priest I thought might be an ally. He was asleep.

The next morning as I walked home from the dining hall after breakfast I heard someone call my name. Our campus was a ghost town at this point—there were no freshmen orientees or summer students yet, only nineteen other orientation leaders and whoever maintains the B and the C on the football field. So no one else was around when I looked up and saw Ian running toward me, much faster than his usual tackling speed. He was still across a parking lot when he started shouting.

"YOU'RE A FUCKING DYKE???!"

He shattered the air with his screams, repeating that question over and over until he was directly in front of me. I'd never seen him so mad—or anyone that mad, really—and I tried to get around him and make it into my building. He stopped me, holding me by both shoulders and screaming down into my face: "YOU'RE A FUCKING DYKE. YOU'RE A FUCKING DYKE." I had no idea how he found out. Maybe it was my speech, or maybe he'd heard about me and Jo from some other source. I thought he was going to hit me. The look in Ian's eyes said *I'm going to beat the shit out of you.* And maybe he would have.

Ian was still holding me by the shoulders when a coworker of mine, Tim, exited our dorm. Thankfully, that coworker immediately saw what was going on, and double thankfully, he was bigger than me.

Tim ran over to us. "Hey, man!" he said to Ian. "You need to let her go." Ian held fast, ignoring him. Tim stepped toward us, moving Ian's right arm off my shoulder and stepping in front of me. "You're going to leave now," Tim said forcefully. "You're going to leave right now." Tim wasn't Ian's height, but he was strong. I don't think Ian was looking for witnesses or an opponent in a fight.

Ian stood there for a long moment, looked at Tim, pointed at me, and said, "SHE'S A FUCKING DYKE." Then he spun on his heel and left.

We waited until he left the parking lot, then Tim walked me into the building and to my room.

"Thank you," I said to Tim as I stood in the doorway, shaking.

"Of course," he replied, because what he'd done is what we should *of course* all do.

I wish this weren't the story of the last man I dated, if you can say Ian and I dated. Or you could say he preyed on me. I'm not sure if he knew better. Like me, Ian had gone to Catholic school his whole life, and was from a conservative Catholic family. Maybe he thought of women as something to be conquered or worn down, that female sexuality was only spurned advances and male sexuality only unfulfilled desires. Maybe he didn't know his partner should want to be with him, too, and to be with him while sober. Maybe he didn't know what real love or real sex looks like. Or maybe he was blackout drunk, too. Maybe all these years later, he hasn't registered what happened that night. Maybe I'm the one who ended up with more clarity.

In 2018, I released a special called *Rape Jokes* in which I told this story for the first time. A ton of amazing people donated their time and space to make the project happen and I was able to offer the special free of charge for anyone to watch via my website, while directing all donations to RAINN (Rape, Abuse & Incest National Network), the largest anti–sexual violence organization in the country. It raised a bunch of money. Doing press for that special—saying the word "rape" over and over again for weeks on end—was grueling and brutal. I'm glad I told this story then and had the chance to write it here. Most survivors won't get the chance to be believed or listened to or publicly supported the way I was. What a fucking privilege, to be exhausted by telling my story too frequently, and how fucking awful that any of this happened to me—and any survivors reading this—at all.

I ask for enthusiastic consent from sexual partners. I don't credit Ian with giving me that perspective.

Consent is a practice I chose. You can, too.

REQUESTS GAY APOLOGY

On May 17, 2004, exactly a week before I graduated from BC, Massachusetts became the first state to legalize same-sex marriage. Like some of your white parents might say with regard to Woodstock or Woodstock '94 (I don't know how old your parents are), I was there, man. Jo and I woke up in the off-campus spot where she lived with two friends and one of those friends's *Catholic gasp* live-in boyfriend and we saw the news on our phones JUST KIDDING PHONES COULDN'T GET NEWS YET. We found out because an owl flew in our gay window and dropped a letter that said, "Dumbledore can legally wed! See you at Hogwarts."

Anyway, we sprang right out of bed after that owl and went to hang with Jo's housemates. She was living a few blocks from campus in this whole fricking *house*, which felt very adult. I'd moved back on campus with my suitemates from sophomore year, a few of whom I was still not out to. Lindsay had since apologized for her silence after I told her about Jo, and I'd also had a drunken twenty-first-birthday coming-out conversation with some of the women I lived with (sorry I puked on your futon, Lauren), but after that, Jo didn't really come up in conversation. I was scared to mention her for fear they'd be disgusted by me—internalized homophobia is real—and maybe they all took a cue from me or maybe they thought she had faded in my rearview mirror. She hadn't.

I spent most of my time at Jo's. Often I would leave my place to "go repark my car" and not return for days. "Cameron's parking her car" became a running joke, code for "Um, where the hell has our roommate been?" One evening we went to a beach-themed party, and the last time they saw me for several days in a row, I was running off into the literal sunset wearing only a coconut bra and grass skirt. So, yeah, that really didn't do anything to dispel the perception that I was a party fiend.

In actuality, Jo and I were nesting hard and essentially taking early retirement. Dinner every night was a box of pasta, boiled up, Prego'd, and split down the middle, which we ate while binge-ing Jo's very-off-campus HBO, two Mirandas in that one episode where she wears overalls, camped out in front of *Sex and the City*, and we dreamed together about a future we had never seen any-one else have. We knew no out queer adults. Our Classic Lesbian Future™ involved both of us being social workers (today Jo actu-ally is one, so partially correct), a French bulldog named Belinda Carlisle, and kids somehow? From somewhere? We were able to be openly affectionate in front of Jo's housemates, so between baby names and investigating social workers' salaries, we even kissed in front of them like totally normative monsters.

Jo and I had attended marriage equality rallies all spring down-town at the Massachusetts State House, taking the train to the Government Center station and feeling a hundred miles away from school. BC isn't an urban campus like NYU or NYU but the fictional one from *Felicity*; it's in Chestnut Hill, a suburb of Boston, and feels more like a self-enclosed community with easy access to a city. We didn't have to worry about running into any-one from campus. Sometimes, we even held hands at these rallies. PUKE but in a good way.

Naturally, there were large groups of well-adjusted, sweet-hearted adults who showed up to protest these rallies with signs like GOD HATES YOU, but it didn't say YOU, it said FLAGS but without the L. Honestly and deeply, from the bottom of my soul, I believe the same thing about "God hates flags" folks years later that I did then: that they are scum, wastes of their parents' genetic material, cowards with neither clarity of conscience nor any value on this earth. Oh, did you expect me to say something kind? Not ever. Rhetoric like that gets people like me to be tossed from our homes, fired from our jobs, and beaten to death. Religious zealotry is a big part of the reason we are more likely to take our own lives, live on the street, and struggle with the aftereffects of trauma. It's not hatred I feel for those sign-toting lizards. It's boiling, metallic fury, poured out on the ground as a perimeter around my queer family. COME AT ME, LIZARDS.

On that particular Marriage Equality Day, though, I saw no detractors. Jo and I sat on the steps outside city hall and watched couples emerge in wedded bliss, hands clasped and held in the air above their heads. We even discussed getting married, and THANK GOD WE DID NOT because twenty-two is just very young for marriage. In fact, I'd recommend not getting married before eighty-seven.

In the time since, I've heard many lgbtq+ folks lament our community's focus on marriage over social issues that are more life-and-death—things like fair housing, access to health care for trans folks, and racial justice—and there is nothing more important to me than pushing for change so that every single member of my queer family, especially those more marginalized than myself, can live freely and safely. And I also remember the feeling of that particular victory, that day watching those couples and feeling safe and protected even if in just one state. It mattered to me. It wasn't everything. It wasn't a stopping point. But it was a day that lifted a weight from my chest.

After returning to her house that day, Jo proposed that, instead of marriage, we attend our class's Commencement Ball together, as if we were an actual couple, which we were. At BC, the fight for marriage equality hadn't even come up. The school's nondiscrimination policy was still the focus. I was scared out of my mind, but after years of secrecy, sobbing, and generally sad/scared behavior, Jo put her foot down. If I didn't accompany her to the dance, we were over.

Of course I fucking went. We wore matching black dresses, for god's sake—mine had a pink ribbon belt and she wore a pink ribbon in her hair. As it turned out, two gay male couples within our friend group outed themselves and went as dates, so there were a total of three same-sex couples in our class of more than three thousand.

In my life with my family, other Catholic nonsense reared its head. I was visiting home when, over lettuce cups at no less than a P.F. Chang's one night, my dad told us that his birth family had reached out to him. The horse statues in front of the P.F. Chang's were like, "Wuuuut?" so my dad said he'd just gotten a call, maybe a week earlier. He is adopted and had been searching for his birth mother my whole life. He was fifty-five when he got the call.

My dad's birth mother lived in Ohio and had gone away to

Chicago to have my father in secret. She told folks back in Ohio that she was taking a correspondence typing course, stayed at Catholic Charities for the duration of her pregnancy, and left him with the agency to place with a Catholic family. After returning home to Ohio, she married the man she was dating, and had five sons with him—my dad's half brothers. Those five sons found out about my dad the year I was born, when she was dying of cancer. It was literally a deathbed confession. She told them that they had a brother and asked them to find him. My dad's had been a closed adoption and the identity of the parents was protected; there was no expectation of reunification for the children. There wasn't even a system in place at the time. The only way you might be able to find your birth family was if they also made an active request to be connected with you. As my dad had kids of his own, he began searching for his birth family, and completely separately in Ohio, his brothers also began searching for him.

I was super close to my nana and papa, my dad's adoptive parents, or, you know, his *parents*. They lived nearby and babysat my sisters and me all the time. My nana let me mix up disgusting batches of tuna fish and cornflakes and like salsa or something and she would eat it because she loved me. My papa let me sit shirtless with him in their hot-because-of-blood-thinners apartment and watch *The People's Court*. They'd both been raised in Little Italy and they used weird Italian American slang words I never heard anyone else use. My nana had bright orange hair and my papa wore bright green shoes and they were both about four foot three and I loved them.

Even their love story was amazing. My nana was the youngest in her family with a crew of older brothers, the group of whom were my papa's best friends. The story goes, my nana and papa hated each other—she was a bookish nerd and he was a playboy. My nana's brothers paid for her to attend college, which is gnarly because she was a woman born in 1912, and that's the year the *Titanic* sank, and almost no women born then went to college, except for, based on the photos at the end of that movie, Rose, but she wasn't born in 1912. Anyway, my nana studied to be a pharmacist and so did my papa and afterward my nana, her brothers, and my papa invested in a business together and opened their own pharmacy. My papa wanted to fill the prescriptions while my nana ran the lunch counter, but she was like, "I have the same degree you do, bub. You run the lunch counter and I'll fill the prescriptions." So they ended up not having a lunch counter. Instead, they got married.

But they couldn't conceive. The thing about being Catholic is, if you can conceive but you aren't married, like my dad's birth mother, well then you've failed the Church. But! If, like his adoptive mother, you're married but can't conceive, then...you've also failed the Church! What, did you think I was going to say you weren't a failure?! Not a chance. Also, the burden is solely on you, women!

My nana tried for a long time. She was forty years old, which was very late in the 1950s to be starting your family, when she and my papa went to the orphanage and adopted my dad, and I was with her when she breathed her last breath, two days shy of one hundred years old, surrounded by extended family, the last surviving member of her generation of family and friends. She hadn't wanted to go to her hundredth birthday party, so she died. That's how powerful she was, and never a failure.

My dad has a sister. They're close. She's adopted, too. They grew up together. And now since that phone call, he also has five half brothers. Sometime after that phone call, they met for the first time, and I've met a few of them subsequently. They don't sound alike. They are not Chicagoans. They are not Espositos. They are only a little bit Italian. But they look so much alike. They are losing their hair in the same places. They have the same eyes. He didn't get to meet his mom—she passed the year I was born—but I've seen a photo of her and she looks like me. Or I look like her.

I never realized until I met one of my dad's brothers that my dad and my aunt look nothing alike. Because they seem alike. They carry themselves similarly. They've known all the same people. They remember their grandmother living with them as children, making wine and sausage with her in their basement, and visiting the orphanage from which they were adopted to bring presents for the kids there at Christmas.

They also remember the fear that came with being different—and finding out they were from another kid who lived on their block. "You're adopted," the kid had said, pushing it out like a slur. Meaning: You're less than, you're wrong.

Two years after I graduated from BC, in 2006, Catholic Charities of Boston decided to close their adoption services altogether because, with same-sex marriage legal in Massachusetts, they had no legal recourse to discriminate against queer couples. They'd placed thirteen children in gay households out of 720 placements in twenty years. And then, instead of allowing someone like me to adopt—someone who, by the way, is literally a product of their adoption program and wouldn't exist without these exact services—they preferred to shut the whole thing down.

About a year after I came out to my parents, during a visit home, my dad took me with him to run errands. I remember sitting next to him in the car in a Walgreens parking lot as he tried to explain how worried he was about me, how I'd ruined my life by being gay.

"You'll never have kids," he'd said, anguished.

"I could adopt," I countered.

"If you're gay," he said, "I could never support you adopting a child."

It was devastating. Even knowing from his own personal experience that adoption can lead to happy, connected families, he couldn't condone the idea of me adopting. He was saying that my faith wouldn't accept my family—but until he found his birth mother, I hadn't realized the Church had basically said the same thing to him.

To be in good standing as a Catholic isn't to improve the world around you or lead with kindness. It's to not be gay and physically intimate with the person you love or to not have been conceived by an unmarried parent or to not have gotten pregnant before marriage or to not be unable to get pregnant within marriage. Also, for kicks: Don't be a woman. Because that's not holy enough for the priesthood.

So the real Catholics are straight men conceived by straight married parents who are also Catholic. Which does eliminate Jesus but who cares.

I have more to be pissed about on this topic.

A month after I graduated, Boston College bought over $100 million worth of land from the Archdiocese of Boston. The money went to pay off the staggering settlements owed to hundreds of survivors of sexual abuse, which is fucking awful and gross. Basically my college tuition bailed out the Church.

BC used to call me and ask for alumni donations. At first I politely declined, because I knew it was students working the phone—I'd had an on-campus job, too, and a few of my friends had made those endowment fund calls. But about ten years ago I finally said, politely, "I'll donate to BC when the school broadly apologizes for its treatment of me and everyone else who went there before me and since who's been harmed by their policies toward queer students." They've never called me again, so I must have made the "requests gay apology" list. I'd still like one.

FLUNG INTO SPACE

The day after graduation, I went to open-call auditions for Improv-Boston, a small improv theater with a cult following where some My Mother's Fleabag alums worked. My audition was about as graceful as my post-rugby-practice, cleats-on audition in college; I had almost no voice because the night before graduation you're supposed to stay up all night and scream at the dawn. But I still got cast in their Friday night TheatreSports company, meaning I'd make fifteen bucks a week pretending to be Emily Dickinson on roller skates or whatever other bookish character the theater's nerd-core vibe brought out of me.

ImprovBoston was a very tight-knit group of about a dozen people per cast, with three casts doing different shows. I had been a college kid working with college kids, and now overnight, everyone I performed with was older than me; I was a year past legal drinking age working with people in their thirties and forties. Two weeks into my new gig, someone did a shitty, limp-wristed gay guy character during rehearsal and I exploded into tears, confessing my deepest, most awful truth. "I'm gay!" I sobbed. "Oh god. I'm gaaaaaaaaay."

Through my tears, I vaguely registered folks being like, "Okay, cool." And "Yeah, we can see your cargo shorts." They truly didn't give a crap. The person who'd done that character asked me,

"Was I being shitty?" I was like, "I think so." And then rehearsal kept going. Two weeks into being a lightly paid pro comedian and comedy had already treated me better than the Church I'd given two decades to, and the parents who, you know, physically made me. And that *totally rocked my world*. I'd had no idea that there was anywhere that being gay wasn't a deal breaker; I was out in the real world on my own for the first time, trying to figure out if anything was at all safe. It's not like I had any queer castmates saying, "It gets better!" It was just this group of straight people not being violently disgusted by me or worried for my eternal soul. My mind was blown.

ImprovBoston was a small operation. Some people taught improv during the day, which was pretty much the only way to afford doing improv full-time. Some had partners who helped supplement their household income, but most had noncomedy day jobs. I needed a second income, health insurance, and housing. So by the time the summer was over, I was also working full-time at a charter high school as a tutor, sort of along the same lines as Teach For America, and living on its campus—which is where I met Claudia.

Claudia, one of my roommates, casually told everyone she was gay right in the middle of orientation as if it was a fine thing to be. She had wild, curly short hair, wore thrift store clothing, and drove an old, beat-up sedan with a nightmare back seat so buried by unpaid parking tickets and empty soda cups, it was almost nest-like. Claudia had played softball at Mount Holyoke, a women's college; listened to Melissa Ferrick and the Indigo Girls; and had a whole group of queer friends from college who DATED EACH OTHER and had all moved to Boston. She and

I had dinner together the first night of orientation, and I nearly lost consciousness when she told me she knew other lesbians who weren't me and my girlfriend, Jo.

After dinner, Claudia showed me one of the episodes of her favorite television show, *Queer as Folk*, which she had illegally downloaded via LimeWire and saved on her laptop. For the first time, I saw two people with penises having sex facing each other. I'd never imagined gay men might look at one another while they fucked, or that butt sex could be loving, intimate, and chosen, like I have since found it to be.

A note about LimeWire: I'M SORRY I STOLE DATA. Well, *I* never did because I don't know shit about technology and still say things like "Make the computer go." But I watched a lot of data that other people stole. I didn't have a TV when I lived at this school, and I couldn't have subscribed to Showtime, but Claudia also had *The L Word* episodes downloaded and watching them turned me from side-view pixelated Mario to 3-D *Mario Kart* Mario. With fireballs. Also when I had Ilene Chaiken as a guest on my podcast, I told her I watched pirated versions of her show before later buying them all on DVD and she forgave me my sin.

Ah, *The L Word*. May I begin by saying, you're looking very Shane today. Yes, the characters on that show are thinner and whiter and wealthier and femmier and more transphobic than any ten lesbians I know, but if you're a lesbian, *The L Word* is a little bit like the Bible in American culture: Whether or not you follow its teachings, you're aware of it. The actors gave it a fucking GO and the sex scenes looked REAL and like PLEASURABLE SEX and the show was MAINSTREAM. My first queer community was the comments section of the online recaps, though

I never had the guts to write anything, and I'd like to publicly thank Sarah Warn for creating the space where I read those. I don't think for one second I would have the stand-up career I have today or have cocreated and costarred in a show about lesbians (have you seen the show *Take My Wife*? It's very good.) without *The L Word*. RIP Dana.

Anyway, Claudia and I started having sex almost immediately. This was problematic for two reasons: 1) Dating within the program was prohibited at the charter school; and 2) I was still in a relationship with Jo.

Our boss found out about us pretty quickly, when our third roommate and her entire family—who'd come to see where she lived—got locked out of our room because Claudia and I were busy having sex against the door.

Whoops.

But we didn't get fired. Instead of firing us, our boss *came out to us*. She helped Claudia move into a different room, didn't report us to anyone, and ended up becoming a huge mentor to me. Perhaps she realized a general "no dating" rule would disproportionately hurt the only two queer folks in the program. Also, it must have been tough to enforce that guideline when she was queer herself, housing was tied to our employment, and I'd been keeping my queerness low-key; she'd essentially be outing me.

My boss seemed much older than me at the time, though she was probably only in her thirties, and she started talking to me about and even showing me some of her life, inviting me to dinner a few times with her and her friends. I met her ex-girlfriend! We had brunch at a gay bar! She even came to some of my shows, laughing along in the front row, and once I drove her back to school in her car because she got too tired to drive back. Maybe that sounds weird, but it felt like trust. She was the oldest, outest, most secure queer person I'd yet met. I loved her then and, fifteen years later, I can't believe I was lucky enough to collide with her. Queer lives are sometimes saved in small ways. She really saved mine.

Jo was living in Boston as well, on the other side of town where she worked at a residential treatment center for juvenile female sex offenders and fire-setters. We weren't broken up but we were far apart emotionally and physically. It took me about an hour and a half by train to visit her, but we set up elaborate plans to stay in each other's lives, like I started teaching improv classes at the treatment center where she worked. I wasn't supposed to use trigger words that could put any of the girls in a bad spot, so naturally I'd accidentally offer "You're on fire!" as praise even though I'd never said that before in my life.

That I was seeing both her and Claudia was more of an open secret than a total cloak-and-dagger operation; I got caught in a lie multiple times, often couldn't account for my whereabouts, and sometimes just openly went from cuddling with one of them to dinner with the other. On Valentine's Day, I gave them both cards, said I had diarrhea, then wandered the streets by myself for hours so that Claudia would be asleep by the time I got home.

By the time I left BC, I had gotten very used to living two lives: one with my friends and suitemates, and one with Jo. In other words, I got very good at lying, or if not outright lying, at least hiding and secrecy and editing. Just as I used to disappear from my suitemates' place without explanation and stay with Jo for days on end, Jo and Claudia were each one whole life I was living. I had a girlfriend I lived with, and a girlfriend I went and visited. It wasn't virtuous or even practical, but it was somewhat doable—at least for a time.

Why did they put up with this? I think we were all afraid of losing what we had. We were so young, and there weren't a lot of queer people around, even for someone like Claudia who knew more out lgbtq+ peers. It was also exciting, all this drama, and I felt like I was getting away with something.

With Jo, our relationship was almost familial. Coming out together included the breaking of many relationships we'd depended on, and we found ourselves navigating a new world together, trying to find new family, new communities. At least this is what it was like for me. Jo wasn't just my first love, she was also the only person I had trusted with all these new details about myself, for years. She was the whole way I understood my identity. I loved her even as I hurt her.

Also, Jo and I were a few years older than most teenagers are when they start dating, and as a result, our age-appropriate experiences were different. She was my first girlfriend—but we had traveled internationally together. She was an emotional support when I underwent a major surgery. We turned twenty-one together. We rented hotel (slash motel) rooms. We got groceries together. We essentially lived together senior year. We were also mostly hiding our relationship since we couldn't be out on campus, which was intense in and of itself. So in some ways we operated as an adult couple—and the additional layer of secrecy and isolation made us rely more heavily on one another than might normally be the case in a first love.

Perhaps if I'd realized I was gay at a place and time when it wasn't damning, secret, and painful, I wouldn't have needed so much from Jo or Claudia. I wouldn't have held so tightly to my first love or required so much bandwidth from my second. As it was, Jo was family. And I didn't know how to give that connection up, even as my attraction to Claudia grew.

I don't know what it's like to start having sex in high school or college with a bunch of different partners. At those times in my life, I couldn't really have casual sex with someone I'd randomly met—who would that person have been at BC, and how would I have met them? We barely had cell phones. And I have still never been on a dating app. Instead, when I started having sex, it was with people who were or would become a very important part of my life.

Still, sex with Claudia involved way less baggage. We'd come out to our boss and been treated with compassion. And I didn't have to hide her from my improv friends, who also knew my real deal. Plus Claudia and I had sex differently than Jo and I did because sex is different with different partners?! You're kidding!

When Jo and I started having sex, there was no presumption of experience on either side. Jo was pretty demure, but I was pretty frank—wanting to talk through and try some different things, even though I still didn't know anything about my own body. I had my first orgasm maybe a year into dating Jo. I hadn't yet masturbated for the first time. Even after orgasming, repeating that process was infrequent because the feeling of edging toward orgasm freaked me out. The closest sensation reference points I had were having to pee, and not cramps per se, but the soreness that comes with getting your period. Both of those were feelings I was not actively trying to evoke in myself.

Now I'm all about masturbation. I love that I can have sex with myself. Big fan of porn. Love a good erotic novel. But at the beginning, I thought of partners as responsible for each other's pleasure, which meant not only was Jo someone I considered family and one of the only people I was out to, she was also the only way I could have an orgasm. Talk about pressure.

A few months after we graduated from college, before I started seeing Claudia, Lindsay got married. By that time, she had realized I wasn't going to change, apologized for the way she'd reacted when I'd first told her about Jo, and asked me to be part of her bridal party as a co–maid of honor. She even invited me to bring Jo as my date to the wedding.

I arrived in Southern California the night before Jo to attend Lindsay's bachelorette party. I hadn't been to Lindsay's hometown in years, not since I'd saved all the money from my on-campus job at the library and booked a plane ticket to visit her the summer between freshman and sophomore years. Our whole freshman year, Lindsay would show me photos of her beachfront hometown and tell me tales of her other best friend, Kayla, a gal she'd grown up with, surfed for Jesus alongside, and brought on every family vacation. "If you could meet Kayla, my life would be complete. You two are the same," Lindsay would say. "You would love each other."

If Lindsay had struck me right away as a total California girl, Kayla was the definitive surf rat. The summer I visited Lindsay in college, we went straight to Kayla's house from the airport and she greeted us at the door wearing baggy men's board shorts and a bikini top, her hair still wet from the surf. She was tall and rail thin and greeted me with "Oh Cam, it's so rad to meet you!" I'd shown up with a blow-out and decidedly un-punk-rock cuffed jean shorts. I could NOT see how Lindsay might find us similar.

Then, Kayla came in for a hug. There was something I recognized in that hug—the way she used one arm to support my lower back while reaching the other over my shoulder. It was the same way I hugged women. Protective. Strong. I hadn't yet kissed Jo or realized I was gay, but I did know this: Lindsay was right. In some as yet indescribable way, this woman and I were the same. Kayla, Lindsay, and I spent the whole week together, hitting the beach and closing down diners and dancing it out at a Christian rock concert. There were times when I felt like I might get along even better with Kayla than I did with Lindsay.

In the years since I'd last seen Kayla, she'd been doing Christian outreach to skateboarders in Europe. When I arrived for Lindsay's bachelorette party, we fell right back into comfortable conversation about our plans as co–maids of honor, 'cause, yes, she was the other maid of honor. The locale for that evening's festivities was an airplane-hangar-size neon-signs-and-palm-trees bar where the night's entertainment happened to be Mini KISS. Now, Mini KISS is exactly what it sounds like: It's the band KISS impersonated by little people. Think full Paul Stanley makeup and full Paul Stanley costume on a significantly smaller Paul Stanley.

I'd just done a shot and Kayla stood next to me sipping a beer when Mini KISS launched into "I Was Made for Loving You." Kayla leaned over to me and paused for a second to take a big breath, like she was psyching herself up for something.

"Lindsay says you're dating a woman," she said, eyes locked on the stage.

"Yeah, her name's Jo. You'll meet her tomorrow at the rehearsal," I replied as coolly as I could, waiting for what I assumed would be some serious surfing-for-Jesus backlash.

"Too bad," she said. "I had a thing for you."

OH. Of course. That's what had always felt so similar about us. She was gay. We were two gay women with the same best friend.

I'd never had a woman say anything like this to me before. With Jo it had been mystery and tears at the beginning. We'd never discussed our attraction before acting on it. To have this blond surfer chick make a pass at me, surrounded by all that neon and all that smaller-than-usual KISS, was too much.

I spun on my heel and turned to face her. "You had *what*?!" I scream-asked.

"A thing for you," she repeated. And then she leaned in and gave me a kiss of her own. Nothing mini about it. As she pulled away, I could see Lindsay standing over her shoulder, mouth agape, finally processing what she must have known at some level all along.

We stayed at the bar for another hour and then went back to Lindsay's childhood bedroom, where we were all to spend the night. A few minutes after the lights went out, I saw Kayla get up from her sleeping bag and creep outside. I followed her. Downstairs in the kitchen, she waited for me.

"I'm sorry about tonight," she said.

"I'm not," I answered.

"Kiss me," she said, and then I pushed her up against the wall. The rest is sexy history, and, yes, this would be a great movie.

In the morning, Jo arrived. She asked me how the bachelorette party had been. "Unexpectedly wild," I replied. I could still smell the ocean in Kayla's hair. That afternoon at the wedding rehearsal, Jo watched as Kayla and I stood next to one another, co–maids of honor, and Lindsay walked through her vows. Later, Jo said, "That Kayla. There's something in common between you two." And there was.

So in case I'm the first person telling you: It makes sense that you'd feel familial toward your first love, especially if you're both part of a marginalized group. You still probably won't stay with them forever, and recognizing that might give you the chance to move on to your next relationships with more grace than I did.

I learned how to hide and lie as a survival mechanism. I made decisions about sex based on opportunity and attraction, not loyalty or kindness. If I hadn't found Dan Savage's Savage Love column and therapy and *The L Word* and internet porn and honest conversation with other people about jerking off and learned how to take responsibility for my needs and tell the truth about my actions, I might still be making the same mistakes. Now, instead, I get to make different ones.

ANCHOR AND KITE

The first time I went to a sex toy store—the only feminist sex toy store in Boston—it was with my third girlfriend, Cody. I bought my first harness and an amazing dildo that I'm devastated to admit that I threw away. Look, at a certain point, that dildo just had too much history. But it was silicone (dishwasher safe! Know your materials!) and fully bendable and sparkly green and EFFECTIVE.

Jo had finally dumped my ass for cheating, and, after a few months of singledom, I had been set up on a blind date with Cody by someone at ImprovBoston. For our first date, we went to a jazz restaurant I've actually performed at since, during my brief career as a jazz comedian. Conversation was *stilted*, as we had pretty much nothing in common, but she was cute and she thought I was cute and we started dating anyway. Like truly dating. It wasn't "I live in community with you and we are going to see each other all the time." Instead, we both had time-consuming jobs and activities outside of work, and made actual plans and set aside time to see each other.

While we were at the sex toy shop, I found a "cast your own dildo" kit, which was of course very intriguing to me. If you have a penis to cast a dildo from, I wondered, why would you not just use that actual penis? I was so curious that I asked the person at the counter what type of customer most frequently purchased the kit. Their answer was military folks, for use when a partner is deployed or away, which is an interesting fact/answer, and as I continued chattering away with the counter person about this and more, Cody suddenly piped up, saying, "I thought they meant 'casting a dildo' like in a play."

Look, I'd had an intense and fraught relationship with Jo, followed by/concurrent with a treacherous and exciting relationship with Claudia, but both matches had *worked*. This was a real moment of clarity: my first experience realizing, *Oh, not every queer woman will be a great match for me.* I mean, WHAT?! I couldn't imagine what Cody had thought was in that box. A tiny sign-in sheet? An itsy-bitsy curtain that the dildo steps out from behind onto a dildo-sized stage? I hadn't yet felt the need to side-eye a girlfriend. Now I did.

And this was helpful. I had to learn that sometimes dating isn't all "how are we going to die together" or "I'm a terrible person for sleeping with you since I already have a girlfriend and also I might lose my job and housing but this connection is irresistible" or "you're the first lesbian who's ever made a pass at me and we have the same best friend and my girlfriend's arriving tomorrow but I like you and this will be an amazing story." Sometimes it's this: "It's very helpful information that you thought this was essentially a puppet-show dildo set, and I didn't know that would be a falling-in-love deal breaker for me. But now I do."

My relationship with Cody led me to create a whole framework for relationships, my Anchor and Kite analogy. Operating outside a system where gender roles are dictated by patriarchy, I wanted some sort of guide for determining who to date. So I came up with Anchor and Kite—and I talked about it so frequently in my twenties that one of my exes got a giant anchor and kite tattooed on their arm as a surprise for me when they went home for Christmas. I found this out at an inopportune time: when I picked them up at the airport to break up with them, my bags in the back seat, since I'd moved out of our shared apartment over the holidays.

Ill-timed tattoos aside, the theory was this: One person, the anchor, holds down the fort, emotionally speaking. They are usually more responsible, rooted in reality, and nurturing. The other person is the kite. They lift the couple up, focus on fulfilling dreams. They are shinier, less resolved, and more open. They fly on the wind. I believed role switching was possible, but that everyone had a natural tendency.

Some of this still makes a lot of sense to me—I respect little Cammy for trying to describe complementarity. But years of staring out various windows listening to the song "Wig in a Box" from *Hedwig and the Angry Inch* (one of my favorite staring-out-the-window songs) while deep in thought have also taught me...I have trouble trusting people. Not like I don't trust people because I think everyone is a secret jewel thief waiting for Sandra Bullock to get out of prison so we can all hang with Rihanna and GET THOSE JEWELS. I don't trust people to like me.

I'm unsure if it was growing up around so much focus on saintly purity or achievement in academics and extracurriculars or if it's just because my family was loud and I didn't always get heard or if it is presenting as masculine of center and internalizing our culture's great discomfort with GASP! mannish women (what is mannish? And what are women?) or maybe it's that I had a thing wrong with my face (crossed eyes) and I always felt ashamed of that or maybe it's latent eating disorder bullshit. I DON'T KNOW WHAT THE FUCK IT IS. Probably all of that. What I do know is that I basically always feel at some deep, deep level that I am a burden and my emotions are a burden and everyone would prefer that I joke from a distance than be a nearby soft slug with feelings. In fact, it's almost as if I contrived an entire career wherein I charge people to listen to me talk about my feelings as an insurance policy that they are not burdened by my totally normative human needs like companionship.

When I'd unfurl my Anchor and Kite theory, I'd always follow with "I'm a kite." I thought this was because I was interesting and hard to nail down and full of potential. I thought shininess would get me adoration and that adoration would feel like intimacy without risk. Comedy made me feel shiny.

After three months at ImprovBoston, I went to an open call for Improv Asylum, the other big improv theater in Boston, and got cast in their main stage company. It was a huge leap from one show a week at the nerdier, artsier ImprovBoston to shows six nights a week at the city's larger, more commercial/touristy option, Improv Asylum.

In Boston, there's no comedy job more lucrative or esteemed than being on the main stage at Improv Asylum. If you want to be a professional improviser, the one way to do that is via main stage at IA. Most people get cast in the main stage after taking classes at one or both of the theaters, then teaching classes at one or both, then working on an understudy team. I'd never taken one class in improv, ever. Somehow (shininess?) I jumped the queue. And I was not prepared.

Main stage at IA was a sustainable full-time job. Which was great—except that I already had one, at the charter school where I lived. All my coworkers at Improv Asylum were working at the theater, and just there, full-time, supplementing their income by teaching improv classes. I'd made a year-long commitment to my school, so I spoke to my boss/mentor and she shifted my day an hour earlier. I worked from seven a.m. to four p.m. at school, then took a train for an hour to make it to rehearsals or shows at Improv Asylum from six to ten p.m. I worked eighty hours a week, had two girlfriends, and never really slept. I was young, a kite, and I had *energy*. Still, I was sort of failing.

Like at ImprovBoston, the other folks on IA's main stage weren't exactly my peers. They were in their late twenties and thirties, which felt like a big age gap. They'd at least had jobs before. I was working my first two simultaneously. I mean, the owners had to call a meeting with me to tell me my shirts were too short—when I gestured, my midriff showed and it was distracting. Apparently I was supposed to perform in professional clothes, not crop tops. No one else was living that "my home is a dorm at my other job and I wash my clothes at the laundromat down the street" life. Also, when my castmates brought up "yes and," literally the most fundamental improv principle, I had no idea what they were talking about.

My Mother's Fleabag, ImprovBoston, Improv Asylum: I got into the first three improv groups I auditioned for on my first try. In my mind, I'd be Amy Poehler–level in about a year. That is, until I saw her perform.

Amy's about ten years older than me. When I began with Fleabag, the *Upright Citizens Brigade* sketch show had already been on

Comedy Central, *Wet Hot American Summer* was being released, and, like I wrote earlier, Amy was beginning to gain attention as a much-talked-about player on *Saturday Night Live*. In college, she was mentioned at nearly every Fleabag rehearsal. Even on days we didn't talk about her, she was there—on television, on our minds—actual proof that one could spend a few years affecting an awful Jamaican accent (I'm sure Amy's Jamaican accent is just fine) in scenes or hopping around the stage as a "Human Tater Tot" and then actually make a living doing comedy. She was the first person I felt even distantly connected with who had a real comedy career, and I knew she had started just like me.

The connection was admittedly vague—mostly *Wet Hot American Summer* quotes and *Upright Citizens Brigade* DVD–viewing parties—until Amy came to campus to receive an award the year after I graduated. The university was honoring her for artistic achievement and asked that she perform with the current members of the group. I planned to attend for the chance to see her live.

During the Fleabag show, Amy was present and captivating, improvising with college students she'd never met under some tent on the quad. She made it seem easy, and perhaps more impressively, she made it seem fun. Later on, at the dinner, Amy went up to accept her plaque and give a short speech.

The moment she began to speak, a cell phone went off in the room. She didn't miss a beat. She picked up the plaque she'd just been handed, held it to her ear like a phone, and answered it. "Hello? No, I can't talk now. I'm at a thing. I'll call you back." It was a perfect, spontaneous, improvised joke for a room of priests, professors, and teenage improvisers sweating through their shirts just to be in the same room with her.

I met and chatted with her for a moment later that night—something about her sneakers—but years later, it's that plaque-answering moment I still think about. I think about making a perfect joke when you weren't expected to make any jokes at all, and how much that meant to the people in the room. I think about how much we all lost our minds at that joke, how proud it made us that we were even tangentially in her orbit.

That might have been the first time I realized why anyone would choose a career in comedy: because you have to. There's a compulsion to entertain—to make the perfect joke when there are no cameras. That's something I'd felt my entire life. I simply didn't understand until that moment. The Midwestern-jock part of me hadn't realized comedy was a career; the brand-new-to-the-workforce part of me didn't realize a career in comedy had to be a full-time job.

Three months after getting hired at Improv Asylum, I was fired. My bosses were kind about it; I really just didn't know what I was doing yet, onstage or off. This is still the only job I've been fired from, and even though I thought it was probably deserved, I felt "I'll show them" enough about it that I kept an Improv Asylum magnet I'd been given the day I was cast on my fridge until maybe three years ago, when I lost it in a move. I do love to *show them*.

Fired or not, I still thought my super-speedy rise through Boston's comedy scene must mean I had some talent. I was six months out of college and had already held every improv job in the city. When IA asked if I wanted to join their understudy team and work my way back to the main stage, I said no. Instead, I went back to ImprovBoston, rejoined my Fridays-only cast, and spent the rest of my evenings taking improv classes as I finished out my year at the charter school.

As I thought through what to do next, I began to look back toward Chicago. Professionally, there seemed to be more opportunity back home. I was considering entering social work school and had my eye on a few grad schools there. And when it came to comedy, Chicago was known as the be-all and end-all: a true mecca for improv. Even folks in the top levels of comedy in Boston had this feeling of ultimately needing to get to Chicago.

Personally, I missed my sisters. They were both in Chicago—Britton about to enter her senior year at Benet, Allyson having recently moved back from Nashville—and I didn't know how long they would still be living there. I missed my nana. Even though things were still weird with my parents, I missed them, too. Chicago's deep-dish siren song called me home.

BIG DEAL EX

In 2006, after six years in Boston, I went home to Western Springs, moving back into my parents' house till I figured out the next place to hang my ironic trucker cap. In the years I'd been away from Chicago, I'd begun my adult life. I had dated my first three girlfriends, worked my first post-college jobs, started my comedy career—and shared none of these things with my family.

Even though I had been in touch with my parents, flown home for major holidays, and spoken to my beloved nana on a weekly basis, I kept my partners and my daily life secret and separate from my family. My sisters both tried to ask questions about how—and who—I was doing, but I didn't really trust their interest, choosing instead to believe the unmistakable distance that crept into my parents' voices if I brought up a girlfriend. I thought my family didn't want to know me.

I try to forget regrets so life isn't mine to miss (yes, that is a quote from *Rent* and yes, by the time I saw *Rent* on Broadway it starred Joey Fatone)—but it does fucking suck that I never came out to my grandmother. I remember the last chance I had and I remember not taking it. It was right before she died, which was eight years after I graduated from BC, six years after I'd moved from Boston to Chicago, and right around the time I was getting ready to move to LA.

I had been in LA dog-sitting for a week or so, prepping for the move, when I suddenly tore all the cartilage in my right knee picking up dog poop. I didn't twist or fall or get kicked by some wild knee-kicker. I just leaned over a little bit to grab that poop and felt a snap and heard a tear. This was the same knee I destroyed in high school tackling someone on the soccer field. Thanks to aging, "tackling" had become "lightly bending to reach poop." The bottom half of my leg dangled off my knee hinge and the pain and swelling were so immediate, I knew right away that I was going to need surgery. I didn't go to the hospital to make sure. The dog even knew. Have you ever seen an animal be worried about you? I called a friend to come stay with the dog and asked another to drive me straight to the airport. I flew home to Chicago, my mom met me at the airport and took me to the emergency room, and I had surgery the next day, which I know is the same thing I said about eye surgery, but I swear this happened to me twice. It'll probably happen a third time, because don't bad things come in threes?

I spent the next week at my parents' house. I needed supervision due to my immobility and the massive amount of postsurgery drugs I was on, and it was a full house: my parents; my then-partner, who moved in for that week to help out; and my nana (who usually stayed with my aunt, but my aunt happened to be out of town). The company was great. The drugs were strong. My knee hurt like a motherfucker.

At the end of that week, my nana was rushed to the hospital. She didn't go easily. She struggled, tried to get out of the hospital bed. She looked haunted and scared. She was a tough-as-shit broad and she fought until the end. Somehow, either because of a freak accident or because my body sensed an upcoming shift in my universe, I had gotten to spend a full week with her just prior to her death.

I was thirty years old. I was definitely a full adult, and my understanding of my sexuality wasn't brand new. But telling Nana seemed impossible in a different way than coming out to my parents and friends. It's already so weird to talk to your parents about sexuality because it implies sex; I couldn't imagine doing that while looking into my grandmother's face. A part of me was afraid she wouldn't even know what I was talking about and I'd have to go into rich detail before, humiliated, diving into a pit of quicksand like Scrooge McDuck dives into money.

But that is doing her memory a disservice. For one thing, Nana had met a partner I lived with, and once asked me, "Cameron, how many bedrooms are there in your apartment?" I was like, "One." And she was like, "Yep. Okay." So...she got it. I still wish I'd been able to say: "Nana, there is one bedroom because I'm gay, and it was really hard at first, but now I'm cool with it and everything is great." I wish I had taken that risk. Of course, sometimes that's the way fear works. The thing you're afraid of doesn't even feel likely, but it's so big and so loud you can't think beyond the "what if?"

Still, yes—she must have known. My nana read the *Chicago Tribune* every day, cover to cover, and she would constantly come up with reasons to tell me about how much she loved Michelle Obama. She'd voted for Barack—and loving Michelle, specifically, should be an indication of a grandmother who can hear she has a gay grandkid. "Hey, it's only one bedroom in your apartment with that close friend of yours? Boy, do I love that Michelle Obama." I think she was trying to give me openings to tell her.

For a while, I wished that my dad would have told her. I'd had to do so much telling since first kissing Jo. It gets easier, yes, but sometimes it also gets tireder. I just couldn't help wishing that she could be intentionally told—not find out by accident—without *me* having to do the telling. I also think about how different it would have been to have a coming-out conversation with a beloved family member once I was firmly on my two gay feet and doing fine— because, at twenty, I really *wasn't* fine when I came out to my parents. I hadn't been any more sure about my future than they were.

My nana died before I was able to figure out a way to tell her directly. Maybe she also died thinking I'd spend my life closeted, or ashamed. We had a distant family member who had lived with a "friend" his whole life, a relationship everyone knew about but didn't name. What if she could have known I would eventually be famously out, that it isn't something I'm ashamed of or have to keep quiet today?

Though coming out to Nana felt like a bridge too far even years later, by the time I moved back to Chicago, Britton knew I was gay. While I was at BC, my parents once called to tell me that nobody would couple with Britton at her middle school dance because everyone was calling her a lesbian; somehow news about me had traveled through the grapevine. She later got more direct confirmation through someone who had a sister who knew me, and her response was to call me and say, "I love you so much! Why didn't you tell me?" My coming out was hard on her not because she felt confused or horrified, but because my parents had barred me from being honest with her and because she'd lived in a home where they openly cried or fought about what she thought was a terrible secret.

It was awesome to be back home, able to get to know the person Britton had become and see her daily life. She acted in plays at Benet and downtown at the famed Steppenwolf theater. She sang in a choral group that wore old-timey dresses like from a *Game of Thrones* era (although is that show now, just on a different planet? I haven't done my research.) and designed her own clothes and had green hair and was obsessed with mastering the looks in pre-YouTube magazine makeup tutorials.

"These are 'pistachio eyes,'" she'd say, cascading down the stairs at my parents' house. I only ever tromped down those. Never even considered gliding.

Seeing Britton's openness gave me hope that I might be able to somehow better integrate my personal and family lives. I hoped that I could have a girlfriend who knew my family and a family that knew my girlfriend, and as a bonus, that maybe that girlfriend would look a bit like *Hackers*-era Angelina Jolie. And I found her shortly before my twenty-fifth birthday. Her name was X and she was a dancer in Allyson's modern dance company.

When I first moved back to town, Allyson was ending a rocky long-term relationship with a dude who just up and lost it. They'd been together for years, owned property together, shared a dog, and then one morning she came home and Julian had decided to trap a squirrel in their front yard, skin it on their kitchen table, cook it in their microwave, and eat it. Now, in case the microwave didn't give it away, they didn't live in some sort of Davy Crockett log cabin, and they weren't frontierspeople roughing it on the Oregon Trail or my mom's dad making it work in Appalachia. They were living in inner-city Chicago, a place not known for wild game hunting. I mean, do you know what city squirrels eat? Tampons. They eat tampons.

Even the microwaved squirrel wasn't the end for that relationship. Julian cheated, lied about it, and then moved into the unfinished, unplumbed basement of a building he owned and began using a bucket for a toilet. This wasn't a mental illness situation. It was a midlife crisis. Julian was a little older than Allyson. They'd recently been talking marriage, and the discussion of future plans/responsibility pushed him over the edge. He didn't want a wife or prepackaged food or a toilet. He wanted to go it alone, answering only to a squirrel and a bucket. Which he successfully set up for himself, and is (maybe?) not inherently problematic in and of itself. It just wasn't my dream scenario for the big sister I adored and whose fifteen-year-old boyfriends I used to actively threaten after zero provocation. If one of *them* had abandoned my sister for tampon-filled squirrels and a crime-scene basement, who knows what twelve-year-old me would have done. But I do know what twenty-five-year-old me would do, which was: Get. Her. Out.

Allyson suggested we find an apartment together, which sounded great to me, since I was living temporarily in my childhood bedroom. Though we'd made frequent trips downtown to gape at the dinosaurs at the Field Museum, go see actual Michael Jordan play basketball, or visit my dad's office, I was relatively unfamiliar with Chicago's residential neighborhoods. Living with Allyson was the perfect way for me to get acclimated with my new downtown Chicago attitude. She knew the city well. She had a vast and interesting group of art friends, great credit, and a fancy corporate day job that helped pay the security deposit on our three-bedroom apartment on the first floor of a two-flat in Logan Square, the Brooklyn of Chicago.

I wasn't a ton of help on the rent front. I was taking classes at Second City, the city's famous illustrious improv theater; had started a social work master's degree at the University of Chicago; and moonlit as a nanny to make ends meet. I also was trying to figure out how I fit into Chicago's comedy scene—because it had a *very* different feel than Boston's.

Nerds are overrepresented in Boston's audiences. The performers are dorks, too. There are so many legendary schools in close proximity; Harvard and MIT are five minutes away from each other and serve two totally different super-smart-people purposes. Everyone is overeducated, socially aware, hyperliberal (socially) while simultaneously being conservative (fiscally). New England: where Democrats meet Puritans. Every joke is basically, "So then Ralph Nader said, 'Dungeons & Dragons? More like splitting the atom!'" While working at ImprovBoston, besides doing my Friday-night TheatreSports show, I also got my street performer's license to do outdoor puppetry with some of my castmates and did a recurring late-night show that was an election; the audience suggested silly platforms for us, and we had to convincingly extoll the merits of peanut allergies or similar before they voted on the winner. See? Nerds.

Also, the scene was pretty split between men and women and there was a lot of age diversity. Not a ton of diversity regarding race, gender, or sexual orientation, but an amount that seemed somehow massive once I started doing improv in Chicago, where the scene felt like a wall of twenty-three-year-old straight cisgendered white guys casually mentioning blow jobs with every breath.

I joined the cast of a midnight improv show near Wrigley Field, where the Cubs play. The audience was indeed full of dudes wearing backward hats, and my castmates (also mostly backward-hatted dudes) based nearly every scene on the suggestion that I give them a bj. That's not even practical for improv, because you're supposed to physically act out anything that's brought up, not just speak in circles around it. I thought, *You know, maybe I don't want to spend my time endlessly miming blow jobs*, which honestly indicated real growth. I'm not sure I would have known that at twenty-two.

Before Allyson and I fled the squirrel-eating boyfriend, I had sat in my parents' den and used their dial-up internet to get a lay of Chicago's comedy scene. I saw listings for lots of improv classes and shows, which I expected, but there also seemed to be a grow-ing community getting press for putting forward arty weirdos and flourishing in crappy dive bars: stand-up.

What's the difference between improv and stand-up? Improv is essentially acting. You inhabit a character and speak in their voice. Also, it's unplanned. In stand-up, you speak in your own voice, from your own perspective. And the jokes are rehearsed, though you'll probably adapt them to the particular show and audience. Finally, improv is for people who play well with oth-ers. Class clowns do improv. They're light, fun, and love goofing around! Conversely, stand-ups are standoffish, controlled intro-verts. We are either the people in class who shushed you because it was our time to speak, or the people who didn't show up for school at all.

Stand-up is also the apex of an adaptive skill—it can suck the figurative punch out of difficult-to-digest information, the literal punch out of someone's fists, or the Hawaiian Punch out of a juice box. When late-night hosts deliver political opinions via jokes, they have a greater chance of connecting with a large group of people. A good comic can relax folks enough to broaden horizons and change minds. For instance, if you grow up in a homophobic world, jokes can push for acceptance by planting the seed of a new idea, like that gay people are people. That's one reason I was drawn to stand-up: so I could make the world safer for me to live in by cleverly introducing myself and my ideas. It's manipulation, used for good! Though it can also be used for evil.

If you are someone who worries about your value—like if you had crossed eyes or feel strangely about your body or still carry the tiniest inkling that you may end up in hell—stand-up provides maximal emotional output with minimal interpersonal risk. If I was a totally balanced, perfectly adapted human, I wouldn't have to charge people to hear about my fears and missteps. I could just tell them to a trusted friend. But who trusts their friends? So thank you for buying this book. Please don't review it.

I didn't know this yet. I just knew I was curious, not interested in what I'd seen in the Chicago improv scene, and looking for a creative outlet.

So I came up with a scheme.

I dialed up my parents' 'net, Googled "top stand-ups in Chicago," and then messaged them on Myspace, explaining that I was a new comic in town and asking if they wanted to come perform at my show. I didn't actually have a show yet and I wasn't a comic. But I *had* rented space in a theater downtown on Wednesdays. And folks started saying yes.

So Allyson and I baked and frosted seventy cupcakes, since

for some reason I thought cupcakes would really seal the deal—I don't know, I guess maybe I thought folks would like the cupcakes so much that they'd also like me and laugh at all my jokes and tell all their friends and come back week after week and then the show would regularly sell out and become a phenomenon and launch my career into outer space?—and after she got out of her corporate job downtown, we drove to the theater in the rattle-trap van she'd inherited from Julian after he'd gone too squirrel-focused to drive. She worked lights and sound; I handed out cupcakes. Then the other comics and I would get up onstage and tell jokes. I didn't realize stand-ups use a microphone, so I invited all the comics to gently yell their sets. Sometimes only ten people came and we'd be sitting there at the end of the night with sixty cupcakes. Sometimes the house was pretty full. We ran the show regardless, and the scheme worked. Before long I'd been baking cupcakes for a whole year, had five good minutes of material, and knew everyone in the stand-up scene.

I quit social work school, got a part-time job, and was a COMIC. Sort of.

I happened to enter Chicago's scene when it was undergoing a particularly significant transformation. In the '80s there was a huge comedy boom where clubs popped up all over the place, from downtown to strip malls in the suburbs, and almost overnight, there were comedy clubs everywhere. If you were a comic, you could make a really good living driving between a bunch of different clubs in town.

Then, in reaction to this mainstream culture, starting in the '90s and running into the early 2000s, there was the alternative comedy boom. The vibe in the traditional comedy spots was two-drink minimum, brick wall behind the comic, and airplane-food jokes. To push back on the mainstream, people started doing stand-up in rock clubs and breaking the form, being edgier. Comics were less Jerry Seinfeld and more Janeane Garofalo.

While clubs had bookers and owners, alternative comedy was more "of the people." There were still producers who threw shows, but a lot of the best rooms were now being run by comics, and that expanded the possibilities in format and venue. "We've got an alternative show thrown in the back of a pancake house" quickly became "Any space with enough room for a microphone has a show! We've recently moved ours from a basement living room loft warehouse to this laundry basket! No cover!" My DIY, mic-free, cupcake-positive mentality was actually totally in line with stand-up's overall trend.

After a year running the cupcake show, I became a producing cast member of the Lincoln Lodge, Chicago's longest-running alt comedy show. I had started hitting open mics, and began auditioning for hosting positions at what was then the only club in town, Zanies. Like every other new comic, I hustled as many spots at other alt shows as I could, sending out texts and calls and emails and hanging in the back of the room with the other comics.

One thing I love about stand-up: It's a trade. You learn by doing it. Maybe this isn't as true now because of the internet and the different points of access it provides, but when I was coming up, there was a strict hierarchy based on experience. You started with a certain "class" based on the year you entered the comedy scene, and learned your way up the ranks, level by level, show by show, skill by skill. You knew who all your peers were and where you stood in the pecking order of classes that came before you. There was a deference to folks who had been doing stand-up longer, even if they started only a year prior to you, and even if you surpassed them at another point in your career. You earned the respect of your peers and the "upperclassmen" by going out and working hard, night after night after night, hitting as many shows as possible. The scene had no respect for dabblers; everyone was expected to bomb when they started. The skill was in getting onstage again and improving, little by little, over time.

When I started in Chicago, Kyle Kinane, Matt Braunger, and Pete Holmes had just left for Los Angeles and New York. Kumail Nanjiani and Hannibal Buress were still in town and performed at my cupcake show, but were a class ahead of me. More than ten years of knowing those dudes later, I still feel like they're my dad's friends.

Some of that is the deference I mentioned, but I bet there's also another thing at play: In my whole class of comics, there was one other woman, Beth Stelling, who's also still making a go of it. Proud of you, dude. There were women a few years ahead of me—upperclassmen—but we weren't really friends. And there were women in my class whose focus included other things, like Lauren Lapkus and Candy Lawrence did sketch, the Puterbaugh Sisters were a comedy duo, and Jena Friedman wrote a musical. Women popped on the scene shortly after me, like Mo Welch and Liza Treyger. But for the first few years, it was me and Beth and we were never on the same bill, because who would book two women?

There was one gay man a few years ahead of me, but 90 percent of the time, when I was on a bill or at a mic, I was the only openly queer person there. Rhea Butcher, Matteo Lane, and Joel Kim Booster came along a few years later, all starting at an open mic I ran at Cole's Bar in Logan Square (I'll get to that).

But starting out alongside maybe 150 straight dudes in the scene? Brutal. Part of that is always true, for everyone. The late nights, the bombing, the humiliation, and the "I can't figure out this joke or how to get booked on this show." Those things are brutal.

But for me specifically, waiting for a four-minute spot at an open mic meant sitting through comics spewing ALL the gay slurs, every imaginable bit equating gay dudes having sex to prison rape, random tongue-in-cheek comments about how marriage equality was going to lead to people marrying dogs, etc. Then I'd get up and try to regale the same audience with tales of my gay, gay life.

This is still sometimes challenging. The biggest bomb of my career was in front of thirty thousand people at an outdoor amphitheater in suburban Chicago. I already lived in Los Angeles and was there as part of this big stand-up tour with about five other comics on the bill. This was a meaningful venue for me—a place I'd gone to see a zillion shows in high school. Like I saw Beyoncé grace that very stage when we were both sixteen, she was still part of Destiny's Child, and Destiny's Child had four members.

I was in the wings, psyching myself up to perform for the biggest crowd I'd yet seen at a hometown venue, when the dude on right in front of me launched into a ten-minute chunk about fa**ots. I don't say that word onstage. I won't even type that word. My rule is, I only use words that apply to me. I don't ever want to be a tourist in someone else's trauma or identity. I'm not looking to flippantly toss around a term I don't understand when it might be the last thing someone hears before they are beaten to death. I take words that seriously. This comic going up right ahead of me did not. He was a straight man, talking about all the times he'd been called the f-word, and it sucked. He got laughs every time he said the word, as he was saying it, not as a punch line, which meant the audience just thought the concept of fa**ots was funny, or the word itself. Either way, wasn't him they were laughing at. It was people like those in my queer family. People like me.

After he said good night to thunderous applause, I walked out and bombed for twenty-five solid minutes. Bombing in front of 30,000 is actually kind of loud. It's not the crickets of bombing in front of 30, 300, or 3,000. They talk amongst themselves.

This isn't what my whole career has been like—literally the night after the one I described above, I killed in front of a similarly sized crowd—but there have been moments like this my whole career. Many times I've heard, as a response to stories like these: "If it's so hard to talk about queerness, why not just talk about something else?" Like what? Like being straight? I have no jokes for that. Every comic talks about their life onstage; it's just that norms like straightness and maleness are invisible.

One positive side effect of always being outside the norm: I believe I had to work harder, be funnier to get the same response as my peers. I had to thicken my skin, and there are few things that can throw me off these days because I've taken so much shit, especially at the beginning of my career. The love and friendship I have with other comics now, a lot of them guys, took time to build. I definitely spent years as an outsider weirdo. I regularly got heckled by dude audience members who asked to fuck me or called me a dyke. Other comics told me to my face I wasn't funny even though NONE OF US WERE FUNNY WE WERE JUST GETTING STARTED. Plus, I usually followed a string of comics who air-humped the stool where we'd all put our set lists, jerked off the mic stand, or used the mic as a dick, so it's not like these were a pile of comedic geniuses.

There were some rooms in Chicago it took me years to break into. I'd watch a dude open mic–er tell jokes once, get booked somewhere that wouldn't have me, and mentally add that room next to Improv Asylum as a magnet on my fridge. Even when I did get in somewhere, it wasn't smooth sailing. Once, I got brought up onstage in a room I'd been trying to play for years with "We're glad this next comic isn't raped and dead in an alley."

So, yeah, after improv, stand-up didn't turn out to be the blow job–less sanctuary I hoped for. But at least there, my time was my own and I didn't have to "yes and" any of the crap flung at me. So I kept at it, but I did not feel like comics were the artistic community I'd been looking for. Thank god I had Allyson for that.

About a month after Allyson and I had moved in together— before I really dove into stand-up, while I was still figuring out that improv might not be the thing for me—Allyson invited me to a dance show. That's where I met X.

I had decided to tag along to see the show and hang backstage before and after to get the dancers anything they might need, like the manager of a high school basketball team, but for dance. I knew most of her fellow company members by then; Allyson had set up the third bedroom of our apartment as a dance studio.

If you've never hung with modern dancers, they are earthy and ripped and all dress in a style I'd call "boho *Flashdance*"— mid-2000s Mary-Kate and Ashley mixed with a Nike running catalog. Lots of off-the-shoulder knitted tops and drapey shorts worn over gauzy knickers. Her company would come over to roll around on the floor and test the limits of pants and I'd stand in the doorway and chat with the gals as they stretched before being pulled into the room and forcibly stretched by them myself. "CAMERON," they'd yell. "Get in here so we can adjust your psoas." Which is apparently the name of a muscle.

I loved the attention and I loved feeling like part of such an offbeat, oddball crew. These weren't teenage ballerinas gunning to dance *Swan Lake* at Lincoln Center, but folks in their mid- to late twenties and at the top of their game, who worked day jobs without expectation that they'd ever be fully able to financially support themselves with dance alone. They'd all started dancing as kids, and now past their prima ballerina teenage primes were artists in it for the art, trying to figure out career longevity without commercial viability. It was the opposite of the comedy hustle, where most folks start in their twenties and race to get paid.

I don't remember meeting X before the show. Perhaps I was too distracted by my own backstage pacing as I took in the stretching dancers, the blue-lit, unmarked art space, and the arriving audience of folks who looked exactly like they'd hang at blue-lit, unmarked art spaces. It was a stimulus overload to see so many new kinds of people. People with cupping bruises! People with tattoos they'd done themselves! And even some people who didn't wash that much but not in an off-putting way!

So while I don't remember X walking in or warming up, I *do* remember seeing X onstage. I remember the specific way her waist twisted as if she were being spun from the inside, and the control she had over her shoulders. And I remember her face as she danced, her so-open black-brown eyes and her hungover Jessica Rabbit lips that seemed to almost stick to her teeth. She looked like a fucking badass, like someone Helena Bonham Carter would eat steak with or like the gal-product that would have been created if the dudes from *Weird Science* accidentally clicked on photos of whiskey and cigarettes during their "We're making a woman!" process. I recognized her immediately. She was my *Hackers*-era Angelina Jolie.

Of course, she was also someone my sister knew, so I decided a bit of postshow recon was in order. Luckily, I was invited for drinks with the dancers and their roommates, dates, and partners at the bar below the art space. I'd have the perfect moment to ask Allyson questions like "What's Angelina Jolie doing both time traveling from 1995 (*Hackers*) and beginning a career in modern dance?" and "Why hasn't she been to our apartment?" I decided to play it cool because I didn't want to seem too creepy.

One thing about perhaps lesbians in general but definitely me: We're not as into straight girls as television and Katy Perry would have you believe. You know what I love? Mutual attraction. You know what I don't? One-sided pursuit. Knowing what it's like to be hunted, I'm slow to approach other gals. Culture has somehow gotten the message that all Kinsey-scale-totally-straight women are gay for five minutes (or five shots) and all queer women are stoked about that, but I'm not *so* into feeling like a compromise, pity fuck, experiment, or professor of queer sex. Well, that's not totally true. I'd love to be a professor of queer sex. I'd spend my whole salary on blazers.

There's also a bizarre (though ever-lessening) stigma around mistaking someone for queer. Why a queer person would feel guilty for this when we know being queer isn't a bad thing isn't exactly beyond me, per se (patriarchy!), but it is a feeling I wish I could shake off. Especially now, when queer looks are part of street style, I wish I could be like, "I'm not sorry I thought you were gay. That is a gay haircut." We will get there! Perhaps straight dude comics could help by universally moving away from that omnipresent gay panic joke that involves the phrase, "I wouldn't suck a dick for one million dollars." And it's like, hang on, who is paying you one million dollars to do something you're bad at and don't want to do? There are many queer dudes who will suck a dick for the low, low price of free, so you're pricing yourself out of the market.

For these reasons, I reined in my top energy and approached X with calculated chill. "That was amazing. You were amazing," I said. "I'm Cameron, Allyson's sister."

"Oh, I know. The gay one, right? I'm X," she replied in a rich, rolling accent, and I was immediately slayed. I hadn't expected her to have an unheard-to-my-ears accent, because in my little hometown, Greek salad was a risqué ethnic food. But X was South African, and her English was perfect, but since Afrikaans was X's first language, her accent sounded a bit like Sharlto Copley's, if you've ever seen *District 9* or *Chappie* or *Maleficent*, wherein he costars alongside ANGELINA JOLIE because time is a flat circle. And if you have no idea who Sharlto Copley is, think Katharine Hepburn doing an impression of Sean Connery. That's X's voice. And it did add an extra something to her mystique. After all, Katharine Hepburn is a dream girl, too. And an Angelina Jolie/Katharine Hepburn/Sean Connery hybrid might be peak white-person hybridry.

I suppose you might ask, "Who is named X? Is that a South African name?" No, not really. "Is it a family name, then?" Nope. Not a family name. It's just her name. And in the course of the next eight minutes of conversation I also found out that she A) worked as a server at a biker bar, B) was the only child of a South African soap star, and C) agreed with me that the *Terminator* films have true artistic value. I believe I would have proposed not-yet-legal-in-Illinois marriage on the spot had X not interrupted me.

"Oh, excuse me. There's my husband," she said, waving a thin, bespectacled bearded dude over to our table. "Cameron, this is my husband, Zach," she said. "We're not together. He's into tabletop miniatures."

"No, we're not together," Zach agreed. "But I do love staging battles for tabletop gaming. You were great up there tonight, X."

Unlike Jo and I, X and Zach *had* married at twenty-two. By twenty-five, they were separated but not divorced. I'd been trying to suss out X's sexuality, and meeting her husband didn't completely answer that question—bisexuality is real!—but meeting her boyfriend threw me off the scent, availability-wise. I was standing there, chatting with X and Zach, when another dude approached. This guy was massive, a heavily muscled six foot four with a shaved head, face tattoos, a black sweater cape, and pale, pale blond hair.

"Oh, Cameron," X interjected. "This is Matthias, my boyfriend.

He does energy work." And then the conversation continued. If you've never stood with the woman of your dreams and her husband and her boyfriend, then you've missed out on at least one very confusing, charged, and mildly informative chat about how to best paint small metal soldiers and the benefits that come with the practice of reiki.

Okay, she's taken, I thought, noting Matthias's culturally appropriated arm band tattoo, *but I've seen* Hackers *enough times to know that friends can also be really valuable in a pinch. I shall try to be her friend.*

I got X's number that night. Our chemistry was so immediate I didn't even ask for it, she just took my phone as our group walked out of the bar together and programmed her number in. "You'll text me this week," she said, "We'll get coffee. I take mine black." It was an inevitability, not a question.

It was never a question with X. She and I had that thing where you make eye contact and see someone's whole past. I knew it the moment we began talking that night after her show. Whatever she saw when she looked at me wasn't my face. It was "my whole thing," maybe? She knew me.

I had worried that Chicago might represent a step back for me, a step closer to my pre-Boston repression. But X was nothing like my past; she was all future. She French-inhaled her cigarettes (you could smoke in bars then), lived off Jack Daniel's and Big Macs, and cursed like a sailor trying to outcurse all other sailors in a game of *So You Think You Can Curse.* The night we met was the first time I found the following two things sexy: McDonald's hamburgers and dark under-eye circles.

She looked perpetually art-exhausted, like she'd been up all

177

night sketching or stretching or both. I later learned this was *her* whole thing. The world, her art, interactions with people on the street—things weighed heavily on X. All things did. She was strong but burdened. She felt *everything*. Conversely, I'd never felt a thing in my whole entire life. I'm a thinker. Well, I'd felt attraction and sadness but I hadn't felt "I saw a bird and that bird looked like the sea and that reminded me of the journey all women are on to discover our true selves and it made me cry." But X did. Like, she *felt* McDonald's. As we walked out of the bar that night, right after she'd given me her number, X said, "Gawd. I need a burger," with all the gravitas of Bette Davis. It was all I could do to not create my own Jimmy Stewart–inspired scene and grab a passerby with a "Don't you know me? You do? Well then, get this woman a burger, dammit!" That's how I always felt with X, like I needed to get her needs met—and, maddeningly, like I couldn't ever meet them.

For days after that first night I stared at my phone, willing the perfect text into my head. *Okay,* I thought, *what says "committed friend who's open to more but respects your boundaries and also your energy worker"?* I decided on `coffee?` in all lowercase to be slick, and then paced around my and Allyson's apartment, LOS-ING IT and hoping my question mark hadn't seemed too desperate. She got back to me an hour later. (This was way back in 2006 when you could respond to texts an hour later because maybe you hadn't looked at your phone for an entire hour.) It was four sentences. No questions. And it was perfect.

```
yes, of course. tomorrow at two. sip coffeehouse.
come by my work and we'll walk together.
```

It was the "of course" that clinched it. Of course I met her for coffee the next day. Of course we chatted from two p.m. through dinner. Of course I went to her place afterward. Of course we lay on her bed facing each other that night and she told me stories about her childhood and I reached out and gently traced the lines of the tendons on the insides of her wrists with my index finger. Within two weeks she no longer spoke about Matthias. Within a month she had left him. She left him because I cried when I told her I knew we were supposed to be together over the phone and because she walked over to my apartment in the middle of the night to comfort me. I met her at the corner, tears freezing on my cheeks, and we talked for a moment. When it began to snow those tiny, glittery flakes that fall when it's too cold for big, wet flakes, she kissed me. It was a kiss we'd started the night we first met, a love-at-first-sight kiss, a perfect cinematic girl-gets-the-dream-girl kiss.

Here is a true thing about love-at-first-sight-type love: It is impossible to sustain. Movies end when the star-crossed lovers finally make it work. Or when they both die. And lesbian movies end when the lesbian who was previously dating a man but now realizes she's a lesbian goes for the lesbian who's known she was a lesbian for the duration of the film. Love at first sight doesn't sign a lease, for example. But X and I did, a year and a half into dating. So I also know what comes *after* finding the woman of your dreams.

GENDER PRES

X and I had been together a few months when Christmas rolled around. Britton would graduate high school in the spring and Allyson was single; we were all home, sleeping in our childhood beds, just like when we'd been kids. The only difference was that I had brought X with me.

Since X was Allyson's friend, my parents already knew and liked her. She wasn't scary to them; in fact, they loved her. She easily bridged the gap between my gayness and my family. This was mostly helpful but also partly bizarre. On Christmas morning we were all in our pajamas opening presents together when my dad said, "X, you're like the fourth daughter I never had!" Having my girlfriend in my parents' house celebrating a super-family-centric holiday was a dream come true for me. At the same time, I was a little like, "You know we have sex, right?" It felt less like bringing a partner home for the holidays for the first time, and more like Buddy Time with Cam and X!

While it helped that my parents already knew X, they welcomed her for more than that reason. Something had shifted for my dad around the same time I moved back to Chicago. He had a total change of heart about my sexuality. I had missed him so much in the five or so years that had passed since I'd first come out. Sometimes I still can't believe that we got each other back.

My dad had the same Catholic upbringing I did, only decades earlier, when I'm fairly certain the Church wasn't *more* progressive. For me, coming out included the irrefutable evidence of my feelings. My dad, on the other hand, basically had to take my word for it; he was taking in this news from a distance, and that made him feel helpless.

For both of us, coming to terms with my sexuality was painful and confusing and slow, but—it was also important and honest and *doable*. I saw him change. My dad is still a committed Catholic, though he attends Mass far less often. He fights with himself over whether to attend out of allegiance to me. The way I figure it, my dad's evolution is a road map for how straight, religious parents can better love their gay children.

Since then, we've openly talked about his process. He told me that my sisters and mom were relentlessly supportive of me and frustrated by his response, and how that worked its way through him over time. He said he had been worried that his friends, guy friends in particular, wouldn't understand. Sometime during the period when we weren't speaking very much, he told two of his closest friends that I was dating a woman. The first was the kind of man who wouldn't tell shitty gay jokes; the other probably would.

The reaction of the first friend didn't surprise him. "Cameron is a great person," he said. "How is she doing with this—and how are you doing?"

My dad was honest with him about his struggle. His friend was very understanding and supportive. "But," my dad told me later, "I *could not answer how you were*. For the first time in my life with kids, I didn't know the answer. That felt awful."

The response of his second friend, the one he was more

nervous to tell, shocked him. "Really?" that friend said. "That's great! I know a lot of great gay people. And Cameron is such a great person. How are you handling it?"

Again—and major props to him for it—my dad was honest. He confessed that he wasn't handling it very well. His friend said, "She's still just Cameron, right?" And my dad told me how that felt: "Like an ice-cold bucket of water right in the old face."

Not long after I'd moved back to Chicago, my dad made a formal apology to me. He invited me to lunch, and asked for my forgiveness over iced teas. He told me how much he loved me. I remember pausing, being quiet. I was surprised and nervous and sad and hopeful. Then I said, "Thanks, Dad. I love you, too. I forgive you."

And I did forgive him. But I also don't know if I've ever been able to let myself feel the full scope of anger and grief that was truly going on for me during the years I felt most rejected. I think it's too scary. My pain was immense—but I also had to survive. I had to keep trying to go to school, be a person, and graduate. I had to finish the day and the week and the month and the semester and the year. I had to forgive my father. What else was I supposed to do? Cut my dad out of my life when he was asking my forgiveness? Drop out of school, when by the time I figured out my school was wrong and I was right, graduation was around the corner? Quit comedy and get some normal job wherein I'd also potentially take a bunch of crap for being queer? Fall off the planet? I guess those were the options. It's not a mystery why the incidence of substance abuse, suicide, and sexual assault are so high in lgbtq+ populations.[3] I got lucky. I drank, I lied, I ate, I hid—and I stayed in my life as best I could.

I asked him, later, what had changed for him that made him apologize. He wrote me an email, which said: *One day I woke up and remembered holding you the moment you were born. I remembered feeding you, changing your diapers, singing to you, playing with trains, teaching you how to make a bow and arrow, cooking together, and many other wonderful moments. I remember it like it was today. I had a lightning bolt thought: "She is still my baby, my daughter, whom I love so much." And I thought, "What can I do to show her that I love her?"* That's when he called.

He added, *Until your early twenties, you were the most devoutly Catholic person I knew. I feel that your Church—my Church—let you down. The Catholic schools I attended all my life did not directly teach me anything about gay people except to dictate that same-sex attraction was a choice. I believe there is a God. I believe Jesus loved/loves every type of person. You are special and I believe—no, I know—that you are loved by God no matter what any man-made religion says. And my sword and my shield will always be out for you. I have your back, your side mullet, and the whole package that is you. Period.*

Here's a true thing: The first time I could vote, I voted for George W. Bush. I grew up around LOTS of Republicans and my understanding of the Republican party when I left for college was that it was the party of small business owners. I'd been taught to be pro-life, and overturning Roe v. Wade and "protecting" small businesses were the decisive issues folks around me voted on. So in November of my freshman year at BC, I went to a rally for the soon-to-be second President Bush with the College Republicans. I held a sign and even shook his hand.

During the 2004 election, just months after I graduated from

BC, my dad and I were still fully in conflict. I didn't vote for Bush again. I don't know who my parents voted for. But four years after that, in 2008, I wrote my parents a letter and asked them to vote for Barack Obama. I distinctly remember the phone call that followed—a phone call they made to me, to hear me out. "My life is literally on the line with this election," I said. "Please vote for Obama. I think this person could be president when marriage equality happens." And you know what? They *did*. They voted for Obama because I asked them to. Two people who cried when I came out—who brought me to a therapist to try to solve my gay problem—voted in favor of their daughter's right to be a human being.

Maybe this story says it best: I called my dad a little while ago from Provincetown, a gay resort town at the end of Cape Cod in Massachusetts. He asked when I was coming home next and I told him the Fourth of July.

"Watch out on the road because there'll be drunks out there on the Fourth," he warned.

"You don't have to worry," I said. "I'm taking a ferry from here to Boston and then flying to Chicago."

He said, without missing a beat, "I didn't know they had fairies in Provincetown." Nailed it. A well-crafted, deftly delivered gay joke told *with love* can totally ring of acceptance. And this did!

So, my first year back in Chicago was SIGNIFICANT. I switched from improv to stand-up, met X, and moved into a zone of real acceptance with my folks, which was a particularly big leap for my dad. It's also when I got my first gay haircut.

When I returned to Chicago, I still had long hair and wore

mostly clothes from the women's section. People didn't know how to place me; men would still ask me out. Then Allyson and I moved to Logan Square, a predominantly Mexican and Puerto Rican neighborhood. There were people of all different ages and races and there were a ton of artists, thanks to gentrification. It wasn't a specifically queer area, but this was the dawning of the hipster age and I consistently saw people who presented themselves with a bit of gender-fuckage. Like straight men wearing women's skinny jeans was cool at the time—this was stuff I hadn't been surrounded by before.

Then there was X. She was in the spectrum of faces and genders that straight cis men really respond to. Like, I think I'm attractive, but I'm on the butch end of the spectrum and butchness only really gets catcalled by shitheads who want to shame me for being masculine of center and outside my house. X was one of those women who gets asked out on dates on public transit or has customers write their numbers on their checks when she's their server.

This is gross, but true: X's brand of hotness bought me status I hadn't seen while moving through the comedy world as a single dyke. Dating her ushered in some new, fucked-up acceptance from my male peers who were basically like, "She's hot. So I guess maybe we have something in common? We like hot women." I was like, "I also *am* a hot woman. But yes."

And there was the way X treated me. She came to see me at shows and sat in the back and smoked—I could always see just the lit tip of her cigarette from the stage—and laughed the loudest of anyone in the room. "You were brilliant!" she said each time, and even when I ate shit, she meant it. She always thought I was funny. Seeing people present in different ways, getting some approval from the comedy dudes around me and A LOT from X, and happening to have a hairstylist who did edgy cuts all pushed me toward my side mullet.

It started subtly—one side just a little longer than the other—but before long, half my head was shaved and the other feathered into a Mrs. Brady flip. Super chopped up, highly stylized, and very recognizable. I loved this haircut. It felt like me. I put up a one-woman show called *Side Mullet Nation* that had an extended run in Chicago. My first ever merch was side-mullet-adorned pins. Even my parents loved it. My dad once made me a giant birthday card using a Xerox machine where he'd glued a side mullet onto a baby picture of me.

I used my side mullet to open every set. I had this joke that I consistently used as an opener: "As you can tell by my haircut, I'm a ThunderCat...and a giant lesbian." Once the audience knew I knew I looked gay, the rest of the set went smoothly. If I didn't acknowledge my appearance, it would be mentioned for me, like this one time when a guy in the front row yelled out, "You look like a woman who doesn't sleep with men!" And he was right. For some people, it's not just disgusting for someone to BE gay, but it's also disgusting for them to LOOK gay, like, "At the very least, would you PRESENT straight? Have some respect!"

Now my hair is all short, and these days, I really connect with the word *butch*, but I don't know that that word describes me 100 percent. I've always felt more like a feminine man, maybe? We have so many words—*dyke* and *tomboy* and *stud* and *andro* and *boi* and *femme* and *futch* and *diesel* and *daddy* and *chapstick* and *fluid* and *queer*—and I connect with a wide array of those descriptors. My gender is David Bowie, full makeup, but also a woman. So, Tilda Swinton? No, that's not even right. All I know is I have this makeup artist I work with now and she lets me refer to lipstick as "men's lip tint" and that feels right to me.

In Chicago, I used a bicycle to get around. Since that meant arriving for shows drenched in sweat, bike wasn't the most convenient or even the most logical mode of transit, but I was a hip person in the mid-2000s—bicycle riding was mandatory. And it provided an easy way to edge my clothing toward funky/masculine. I zoomed the streets in a vest, several neck kerchiefs, jorts, and fingerless gloves, looking like Stevie Nicks guest-starring on *High Maintenance*.

One early-spring day in my first year of dating X, I was riding in the bike lane (wearing a helmet and generally following all the rules) when a woman popped out of a hidden driveway and broadsided me. I broke the driver's windshield going through it face-first and smashed my knee so hard against the car that it left a dent. Cops came. She was ticketed. I was taken to the ER.

Six days later, six blocks from where I was hit, X was hit by a car on HER bike, this time from behind, and she broke that windshield with the back of her head. I went to the emergency room on crutches, with facial stitches, still totally fucked up from my collision, like, "Hey, I'm here to pick someone up." The nurse led me back to where X was getting staples in her head with a real "Who are you people?" attitude and I think I whispered to her, "Stuntwomen."

By that time, X and I were living together in the one-bedroom my nana would eventually ask me about. My time living with

Allyson had come to a close shortly after this one night when, at around three a.m., as X and I slept naked next to each other on my double bed in my completely undecorated and unfurnished-except-for-a-dresser bedroom, the door flew open and the light snapped on. Suddenly, we were awake, staring at my sister's also naked body as she berated me for leaving my unwashed dishes in the sink, and that's too many naked people for me.

So X and I started looking for apartments.

I'd never shared a mailing address with a partner, or really even hunted for an apartment. Just looking for spots with X was exciting. I kept wanting to pull the sketchy Craigslist landlords aside and be like, "I don't know if you realize, but she wants to move in with me."

We found a tiny cubbyhole that cost $600 a month, utilities included, and moved in X's plentiful detritus and my almost nothing. X had enrolled in fashion school and a classmate gave her a dozen empty wooden picture frames and we hung those on the wall and we were home. My first home with a lover.

The night X was hit by a car, my parents met us at our apartment and brought us pizza. My sisters came, too—Allyson after work and Britton straight from the college where she was taking classes a few miles away. And, overnight it felt, I was an adult hosting my family at my home, nursing my partner, worrying over her health, and recovering alongside her.

It was a long recovery. I got the stitches out of my face, and that healed quickly. My back had gotten pretty messed up, though, and after an ER visit, physical therapy, pain med injections, and an MRI or two, I owed $40,000 in medical bills after insurance. While I did have a sizable number of crumpled-up drink tickets in all my jorts pockets, since that's how you get "paid" in early stand-up, I did not have $40,000 in the bank. I did have a lawyer for a dad, and with him came information, resources, and a good referral for representation. I knew that the person who hit me had been totally at fault. I knew her insurance would cover my bills if I sued her. I knew I'd otherwise be financially fucked for years. So I sued.

When it came time to go to court, my dad recommended that I wear a dress. I hadn't bought a dress in a long time, but I also didn't own a suit, and a dress was shorthand for professional attire, so my dad took me to Target and helped me pick out one dress that I wore for the full week of the trial, switching out the cardigan I put on top.

I'd worn dresses for formal occasions growing up; my high school prom dress was a ball gown with boning in the corset that I paired with elbow-length gloves, because I am a beautiful princess. The only formal event I went to in college was Commencement Ball, where matching black dresses was as far outside the box as I could think.

One of the last times I wore a dress was to Allyson's wedding, where both Britton and I were maids of honor. I knew by then that I didn't feel like myself in dresses—Allyson even asked me if I wanted to wear a suit, because she's really just the greatest—but I wasn't ready to feel so visibly different. I also didn't know where to look, what other options there were. It seemed so much easier to just go to Nordstrom with the other women and choose whichever dress was most cut like a vest, especially because we were all able to pick any dress within a certain color palette, so the options seemed expansive enough. I had begun experimenting with other formal looks—I did wear a bow tie and vest to her rehearsal dinner—but I was still in a place in my life where I was almost waiting to be granted permission to look like myself.

Having worn uniforms through high school, I never really had to make regular clothing decisions on my own until college. When choosing an overall style at BC, I went with sloppy: jammies, baggy sweatpants, Umbros, ill-fitting jeans, sweatshirts—a lot of body-hiding stuff. Jo and I had presented similarly—long, one-length hair and 2000s athletic clothing—and I didn't yet have enough comfort in my own gay skin or sense of what queer clothing options there might be outside of that. When I graduated and started working at the charter school, I wore khakis and button-downs, essentially picking back up from my high school uniform look.

It was with my third girlfriend in Boston, Cody, that I felt okay experimenting with masculinity. She was very East Coast femme, and it was as if her femininity gave me permission; having this person with me, I felt more able to break the "rules" simply because she didn't. I started wearing longer shorts. Shorts length is specific, since it inherently involves showing off your legs. Shutting off that offering by wearing shorts to the knee is a real, intentional choice.

And so is wearing a dress to court. I testified in a dress, with my totally strange, punk rock haircut gathered into a tiny nape-of-the-neck ponytail that made me look like I was fighting in the Revolutionary War. It wasn't an actual jury of *my* peers, by the way, partly because no one else seemed to be dressed in drag with a straight-up colonial soldier/Founding Fathers hairstyle. I wasn't in imminent danger sitting up there, of course, but I was scared.

This was prior to nationwide marriage equality, but during the thick of the fight. Many states were passing laws *against* marriage equality—the Prop 8s of the world—and homosexuality was in the news every day. I was unsure how twelve random strangers would feel about me as a queer person. Though I had been somewhat successful shifting my look toward normativity, I still had to disclose during my testimony that I was dating a woman because one of the questions was about my living situation, *and* I had to stay likable while doing so because they needed to believe me. On the stand, you're not allowed to speak directly to the jury at all, and they're not supposed to give you any encouragement with any sort of reactions or body language—not even a smile. I outed myself to blank stares, mentally pleading, "Please think I'm a person."

I won the case, got my medical bills covered, and was eventually able to move to Los Angeles partly because I didn't have hit-by-a-car debt with which to contend. I have no way of knowing whether the jury would have found in my favor if I'd worn the menswear I sport today. I hope so, but very often when I travel I hear from queer folks who can't or don't want to "pass" to feel comfortable at work, live safely in their communities, or simply to survive. Hell, it is official White House policy under the golden toilet administration that women wear dresses to greet the president. And then there are the queer and trans folks who can't or won't "pass" and end up in mortal danger going to the grocery store. Maybe, just maybe, everyone should be able to wear whatever the fuck they want to appear in court, go to the grocery store, or greet the president (or ignore the president), gender norms be damned.

When the trial was over, each one of the jurors shook my hand as they were leaving the courtroom and wished me well. I stood there, mouth agape, like Erin Brockovich when her boss gives her two million dollars, except I didn't get two million dollars and my hair isn't curly.

WOMEN IN COMEDY

In 2010, four years after I started doing stand-up, Sarah Silverman played the Chicago Theatre. I was a huge fan of hers, having somehow seen her first big special, *Jesus Is Magic*, during its movie theater run? I use a question mark there because that's not how comedy specials are released, but that one was. I also loved her Comedy Central show and she was touring promoting a book she'd just published and I'd already read. So I got tickets to her show—good seats, too. They were expensive and I could only afford shoes from Payless that would lose their soles after one week of wear, but I happily saved up for tickets and walked in to see her, wearing my best bottomless shoes.

A lot of comics talk about Carson, Letterman, or Conan (it feels confusing to say "O'Brien") as early influences, but I didn't really connect with any of the late-night hosts or comics I saw on TV. I didn't yet know about Kate Clinton, Karen Williams, or any of the first generation of out lesbian stand-ups. Growing up, I loved comedic actors like Lucille Ball and Carol Burnett, and I think those women are two of the reasons I have a job today. (I once humiliatingly cried this *at* Carol Burnett outside an airplane bathroom. She was nice about it.)

In college, when I found Ellen and Margaret Cho, I was like, "Oh! Stand-up is funny." Margaret was the first comic I ever saw live, and she was so good that a year or two later, when she released a book, I contemplated bringing a bottle of wine to her book signing. "What if I hand her the book and, because of the way I hand it to her, she can tell I *really get it* and then she's like, 'I'd love to seal our close intellectual connection with a toast, but there's no wine!'" In actuality, Margaret signed the book in two seconds and I've since gotten to know her a little bit and I'm extremely glad I didn't offer to uncork a bottle of Two-Buck Chuck back at that bookstore.

I think Sarah was the second comic, after Margaret, I paid to see. I saw other big names as they passed through Chicago and played venues where I knew the bookers/owners. Or when I opened for them. And I think she might have been the last comic I paid to see, unless you count Trixie Mattel as a comic, and I don't. I count her as a comic/musician/queen/planet/star. Anyway, sitting in the audience at the Chicago Theatre, I was stoked. Sarah was fantastic, as was her opener, Todd Glass. Later, they'd both regularly play the show I used to run at the Upright Citizens Brigade Theatre in Los Angeles, so I can also say they *are* fantastic.

That night, after Sarah *crushed*—she truly destroyed—they opened it up to the audience for a Q&A, and the very first question—from a man who was probably sixty-five years old—was whether or not she shaved her pubic hair. He asked this question in front of three thousand other people.

Three years prior, in 2007, around the time I went through a lady's windshield with my face, *Vanity Fair* published an article by Christopher Hitchens entitled "Why Women Aren't Funny." Today, this column would be diluted by the immediate concurrent publication of "16 Pictures Proving Women Aren't Funny

(With Puppies)" and "Women Aren't Funny but You Won't Believe What's Not Funny Next" and a "Which Unfunny Woman Are You?" quiz. But 2007 was the pre-clickbait era. Incendiary magazine articles could still brew up a Stormnado (when Storm from the X-Men makes a tornado), and this one did. Hitchens's points were debated on every news medium—TV, newspaper, magazines—alongside statements made by professional female comics on the topic. That's right: Women who were funny for a living were asked to take time out of their workdays to con-firm whether they thought women could be funny for a living. On CNN or similar. I don't specifically remember a farcical Ghost-busters logo with the ghost replaced by a picture of Lucille Ball stuffing chocolate in her mouth, but that was the vibe.

When this article came out, Chicago was a full-fledged stand-up boomtown where, as you already know, I was one of like three women in my generation. After the article appeared, my phone started ringing. Or maybe the inquiries came in via email, but ringing phones (and rain and rowboats) are more romantic. Either way, the content was the same: I began field-ing questions on behalf of my entire gender. The subject lines probably read: "RE: you and everyone like you—funny?" I was asked about doing stand-up professionally, which I didn't yet do; whether I hated my fellow male comics (I don't hate male comics; I hate men. Jkjk [am I?]); and whether it was ever uncomfortable to tell jokes while on the 3 side of a 3:150 ratio. And repeatedly/ constantly, I was asked if women could be funny.

I was the opposite of easy breezy Covergirl, sweating it out at mics across the city, and the first time I heard from anyone in media or the press was to answer whether I had the biology to succeed in this biz. To make ends meet during that time, I worked nine thousand jobs, including server/actor at a murder mystery dinner theater, nanny, law clerk, tutor, one of those people who hands out new kinds of granola bars in train stations with a "Start your day right with this new granola bar!" and a talking vending machine on Navy Pier. I ate only black beans and Fritos, because that's what I could afford. I rode a crappy ten-speed bike tens of miles a day between work and shows, and when that bike got demolished by a car, got a new crappy ten-speed and rode that one. I ran my own show and joined the producing cast of two more. I don't know if I have the biology for stand-up, but I have the constitution.

And I know comedy is subjective, but I'm funny. It's not up for debate. You either agree with me or you have a bad sense of humor.

If the following sounds self-congratulatory, rest assured I have done many awful, stupid things. I stay up nights mulling those things over and hating myself for them and worrying that murderers will invade my house and kill me. Or that murderers invaded my house while I was out doing so many shows like a hero, and are already in my closet, awaiting my return. And like Tony Soprano, I have weaknesses: I can rarely cry when it would be socially appropriate to do so, I have never been truly happy with my body, and milk makes me very sick. But there is at least one thing I have done that I am truly, openly proud of, and it's that after years of answering the same questions and having the same fights and conversations and wondering about the deficits of female comics in my city, I decided to try a social experiment. I decided to try to flood Chicago's stand-up scene with women.

One thing about me: I am not really afraid to see an opening and create something new. Like when I moved to LA, Scott Aukerman was ending his long-running *Comedy Bang! Bang!* weekly live show and the Upright Citizens Brigade was looking for a new show to fill the spot. I'd been in town for four months but I had MOXIE, so I emailed a friend of a friend who owned a comedy record label and pitched an idea for a stand-up podcast, then we went to the UCB and pitched the show to them. Ryan, the record label owner, was like, "I'm not sure this will work but I'm intrigued," and the UCB was like, "We're not sure this will work but we're intrigued." That show ran for six and a half years—five and a half years with Rhea Butcher as cohost—was called *Put Your Hands Together*, and you can still listen to the podcast.

Back to Chicago. Even just a few years in, I realized nothing creates stand-ups like exposure to stand-up. That was, after all, the biggest reason for Chicago's stand-up boom. With new shows, more people realized stand-up could be an option and started doing it as well. The new comics created more new shows and those shows created more new comics and so on. Most humans need to see that something can be done before we think we can do it. I'd needed to see my first boss and her community be out and okay to think that might be possible for me. So I thought that if women could see other women doing stand-up, more would start doing stand-up themselves, and some of them would stick with it. More female comics would mean a wider range of style, writing, and delivery, and a larger chance that any one of us would succeed, and that some of us—perhaps equal in percentage to male comics if not in number—would be deemed funny.

So three years into my stand-up career, with my cupcake show and the Lincoln Lodge under my belt, I went to the fella who produced the Lodge with a proposal. I asked him to let me teach a class that would help get more women onstage. Not a stand-up class, really. You can't teach stand-up. Stand-up, like surgery, is a skill you learn by cutting somebody's heart out. But you can model confidence and teach joke writing. You can convey possibility.

The course goal: write a five-minute set. I brought in writing exercises I found in books and created some of my own. I assigned homework. Students told jokes aloud in class and did punch-up for one another. I'd give notes on keeping topics personal and delivery strong. And I only had one rule in class: No apologizing. If a student got up to practice what they'd written at the front of the room and apologized or added disclaimers during any part of the set, they simply sat back down to reset, stood up again, walked to the front of the room, and started fresh.

At the same time, I was making my first real solid friend in the stand-up scene, this great Chicago comic named Adam Burke. Adam was older than most of the other new comics, at an almost-fully-in-the-grave thirty. He was Irish, like from Northern Ireland, and whip-smart. He used ten-dollar words in his act, and one night, after giving me a tag for a new joke I was working on, he gave me his number. We started watching action movies together and talking about women.

A buddy I knew through the dance world opened a bar in Logan Square and asked if I'd host an open mic there, and I brought Adam on as cohost and invited the women from the course to try their writing onstage at the mic. They had to sign up and wait like everyone else, but they could come in pairs or as a group, and they'd never be the only women in the room because I'd be there.

At the end of eight weeks, I hosted a graduation show at a real venue in front of a real audience, recommended some additional open mics in the city, and from there it was up to them.

This course still runs today in Chicago. It's called the Feminine Comique and after I moved to LA was taught by my successor, a comic named Kelsie Huff, who went through the class when I taught it despite already being a working comic, producer, and solo performer. Now it's run by another great stand-up, Alex Kumin. In my time teaching, more than one hundred women wrote their first five minutes. Under Kelsie and Alex, hundreds more. Some of these women were never hoping for a professional stand-up career—they were pastors (or priests in non-Catholic churches) and corrections officers and marketing executives looking to try something new and challenging. And some of those first one hundred stuck with it and became professional comics.

Many of my students came to the open mic Adam and I hosted, and because they were there, a bunch of female comics unrelated to the class started out in that room, too. Some nights, half the comics on our sixty-comic list would be women. Half! And it was a great mic. It regularly drew packed audiences and won awards as the best in the city. Ten years later, it's still going strong with new hosts and new comics. In short, my experiment worked. And it gave everyone in Chicago a practical answer to a philosophical question. It turns out that the best way to decide whether women are funny is to encourage a bunch of women to tell jokes.

And how do you do that?

Make space.

Women are cultured to not ever take up space. We apologize, we literally shrink our bodies, we lower our voices, we compromise and try to agree when challenged on a point. All of that culturing is antithetical to stand-up comedy, where you have to be big and loud, take up an entire stage by yourself, guide people through your own viewpoints without inviting a dialogue, and dominate a certain amount of time and space. I knew right away that I was filling a need because in the first session I ever taught, *none* of the twelve women there wanted to do comedy for a living. They wanted to give better sermons to their congregation, to be more commanding at work, to nail presentations, or to have more self-confidence with a physical change, as in the case of one woman who had signed up after losing her leg to cancer.

Here's another thing that is true: Men don't have to be attractive to be looked at onstage. There are some pretty boy comics, whose looks are sometimes part of the appeal, sometimes a hindrance. They sell tickets because they're nice to look at, or because they know they're nice to look at and they joke about that in a self-effacing way that makes audiences love them more. More common are nondescript dude comics and guys that fully lean into what is perceived to make them gross. I've seen tons of men take off their shirts and that's the whole joke: "What if I had THIS body?!" But there isn't an equivalent for women in the stand-up world to the dude who takes off his shirt, demanding that the audience see him.

And, by the way, sometimes women don't even *want* to be seen.

Being a woman or a lesbian or a lesbian woman onstage isn't so different from being one offstage: objectification and sexualization can happen at any moment. Like once, X and I were walking past this rad Boystown nightclub called Berlin after a show, sober and at closing time, when we saw a man leave the club and briefly crest in the doorframe before turning to his right, left, and then falling directly on his face. It might have been funny, except he knocked himself out cold, broke his glasses, and started bleeding from the head. Everyone else leaving the club at this time of night was so drunk or drugged out that they were just stepping over the body, looking at their phones like, "Oh man, if only there was some device I could use to call for help for this guy...Yeah, hi, pizza delivery?" So I stepped up and called 911.

X and I were waiting for the ambulance to arrive when a different dude rolled up on a skateboard. He popped his board and said, "Hey, I think I saw what just happened here. Did you call 911 for a stranger?" I said yes. He said, "You're a good person." I said thanks. He said, "Is that your girlfriend over there?" I said yeah. And he said: "Oh, well, do you think the three of us could...you know?" Seamlessly transitioning the conversation into a proposition for a threesome.

I applaud this man's sense of timing. I like to think he was rolling up on his board and took a moment to assess the situation. "What's going on here?" he asked himself. "Two lesbians in a committed relationship and a guy bleeding out on the sidewalk? Now's my moment! Are we on a busy street? Great. Will an ambulance arrive soon? Fantastic. Are there bodily fluids available from a fourth party not even involved in the threesome? Perfect. They're good people."

By the way, even if we had said yes, how did he think he was going to get us out of there? He was on *a skateboard*. Did he think I was going to say to my girlfriend, "You climb on his shoulders. I'll ride on the front. Let's go!" I told this story at a show once and finished by saying, "And we did it." A guy sitting in the front row turned to his friend and very loudly asked, "Does that really work?" (No. The answer is no.)

In my experience, being a woman or a lesbian or a lesbian woman means fielding unpredictably timed propositions and questions from men. And being a comic just means those propositions and questions are more public (like Sarah Silverman getting asked about her pubic hair in front of three thousand people) or that the person proposing or questioning feels more invited. After all, the comic is onstage talking, sometimes even about sex (all comics except the ones who only play churches talk about sex). She wants that interaction, right?

Like once after the show, an eighty-year-old man asked me if he could will me his collection of soft-core pornography. I had been talking about my life—having a girlfriend, moving in with that girlfriend, whatever—and for some reason, that made this particular senior citizen want to *Mr. Deeds* me his personal spank bank. (Honestly, I wish I'd taken him up on it so that tours of my apartment ended with "And here's where I keep my large endowment of large endowments.")

So that's what it's like when I talk about nothing overtly sexy. But other nights I do cover sex. Like talking about how internet porn keyworded "lesbian" isn't my jam—the fingernail length tends to throw me off and I don't prefer how they always seem to be performing for an off-screen dude. I actually love gay male porn, because their erections seem to indicate some level of interest and agency on their part and because the performers more often seem into each other.

Once after I mentioned my interest in watching two dudes together, a newer comic who'd gone up before me and done a pretty unintelligible set that seemed to focus on his affinity for thick butts while generally lacking punch lines yelled out, "Oh no! Nuh-uh! No way!"

I stopped and asked him, "What? You don't like me talking about two dudes?"

"Yeah," he said.

"What makes you think you get to have an opinion?" I responded.

I can't remember what he said back. Some nonsense about how gay dudes gross him out, but two women? He'd "like to get in on that, just mix it up like some gumbo."

This was another *comic*, gumboing up my set. A comic newer than I was, with less standing, who'd gotten less laughs, fucking with me. I tore into him for a while. Nothing too cruel. But the thing is, he couldn't seem to stop. He never apologized or backed off or understood what I was saying. And after the show, all I felt was that I'd wasted my time onstage on him.

I think this is why women who do comedy hate getting the question "Are women funny?" or its offspring, "What's it like being a woman in comedy?" We don't want to waste our time justifying ourselves to the world's Christophers Hitchens (like attorneys general). We want space to tell jokes. Not more space than anyone else. Just the same set length everyone gets at the mic. We want to be asked about our art, not our bodies. And we want the chance to build careers and perform for the folks who saved up for tickets to see us.

We just want to do the work, if you'd please get the fuck out of our way.

WHAT'S LEFT BEHIND

Right before New Year's 2009, X's visa ran out. She'd never applied for a green card after marrying her husband and didn't want to now that they were separated. Instead, she applied for this super-prestigious specialty O-1 visa for "Individuals with Extraordinary Ability or Achievement"—basically a MacArthur Genius Grant for immigrants—but didn't get it. As this was prior to federal marriage equality, whether she divorced her husband or not, there was no way I could keep her in the States on my own.

She left, returning to Cape Town and a country she'd never lived in as an adult.

I didn't have "follow her to Cape Town" money, and besides, my stand-up career was in Chicago. I hated that this was true, but when you find the person you think you're supposed to be with around the exact same time you find the thing you think you're supposed to do, a decision is required. One has to prioritize. I chose a now slightly less openly hostile set of male peers and my improved going rate of drink tickets *plus* twenty bucks per set, which ended up getting me to her anyway.

Mark Geary, the comedy booker who produced the Lincoln Lodge, where I was a producing cast member, offered me the chance to do a short tour in England. I'd be paid basically the exact cost of a ticket from Heathrow to Cape Town International

Airport, and so I went, bombing for ten solid days in UK rooms before hopping a twelve-hour flight and being picked up curbside by X and her glamorous actual soap star of a mother, who smoked indoors and had a cat with a heavily scarred face and wealthy parents whose house had a name, like out of *Wuthering Heights*.

I stayed for a month. X introduced me to Bovril, a meat spread she used to make meat toast; professional rugby; and this beach where there lived a natural population of penguins.

One morning X was like, "What do you want to do today?"

I said, "I don't know. What do you want to do today?"

And she was like, "Penguin beach."

Nothing in American culture prepared me for the possibility that penguins might swim up from Antarctica and decide, "Let's stay here, in Africa." I had assumed all penguins lived at the North Pole with Santa or at the smelly, now defunct seabird house at the Lincoln Park Zoo.

We met up with a whole crew of X's friends at the beach and one of them had brought along a pal X didn't know and that person was Kristanna Loken, the actor who plays the female Terminator—THE TERMINATRIX—in *Terminator* 3, a character I respect because her arms can turn into guns and knives, but in the film, when she is pulled over by the police for speeding, she makes the decision to enlarge her robot breasts and sexy herself out of a speeding ticket. I like that she's a lady with a wide range of skills.

So there I sat on a rock, in South Africa, surrounded by penguins, hangin' with my beautiful girlfriend and the woman behind the Terminatrix. Did I mention I owned her action figure? Before long, the entire group save my never-braless-in-public D-cup ass had taken their bikini tops off and flitted into the water wearing only bikini bottoms, including Kristanna. Yeah, each Terminator film features its Terminators time-traveling in the nude, but you don't expect you'll ever be able to verify the accuracy of that nudity with your own non-scanning human eyes.

At the end of the day, Kristanna gave X and me a hug as we left the beach. She hadn't put her top back on before doing so. And so that day became Topless Terminatrix African Penguin Beach Hug Day from then until forever. Afterward X and I didn't talk for about two hours. We stared at each other. We ate some Bovril. We stared at each other some more.

Sometimes the zenith of a relationship happens and you know it. You're aware that it will never get better. And that's what this was. I felt the last gasp of our possibility. Because that moment was perfect but nothing else was. I chose stand-up, not a new culture, new language, new home. I kissed X and her mom goodbye (though not both on the lips) and got on a plane with the four sentences of Afrikaans I'd learned and without the person who'd been my supposed forever home.

X's departure from our apartment had been so swift, she'd left everything she'd accumulated behind, and for months, I stayed up nights surrounded by her things. It wasn't until I started regularly dosing myself with brownies procured from a pot-baking friend that I truly slept again, and even then it was fitful sleep. I have a memory of visiting my little sister at her dilapidated college apartment, where she had no hot water, and lying in her bathtub as she warmed water in a four-cup pot on the stove to dump around me by the potful. That's how I felt overall: like I was submerged in a pretty cold, mostly empty tub.

X ended up being in South Africa for most of the next year. I was devastated. We were together and open for a while, but the loss—without any guarantee of her return—was too excruciating, and eventually we broke up for good. X did come back to the States eventually, but not to Chicago—to New York for grad school. We stayed in touch. We're still in touch.

One night early on in our relationship, before we had moved in together, X and I made a list of things we wanted to do before we grew too old: road-trip to Graceland and make a full Thanksgiving dinner and have a pet fish and buy a house. Sleep under the night sky and start playing Scrabble together and visit Paris and get a plant. We did some of them. Not all.

X was my first big deal adult relationship. Then, she was my first big deal adult ex.

Shattered from our breakup, I didn't know what to do next. So I joined the circus.

BIG TOP WORLD

No, I'm serious. I joined the circus.

I was girlfriendless, back in Chicago, and taking any gig I could get. I hosted street festivals where not one person in the outdoor audience was listening, entertained a bachelorette party of six women I didn't know over brunch, and opened for my sister's modern dance company at illegal art speakeasies. And I became a circus ringmaster, which honestly, 10/10 would recommend.

How'd I become a ringmaster?

I jumped aboard the slow-moving CIRCUS train as it rolled through town and that's a lie.

In reality, I convinced this videographer to partner with me on a series of videos featuring the toughest women in Chicago—a feminist sex toy store owner, a fire eater, and, upon the recommendation of pretty much every modern dance gal in Chicago, Shayna. Shayna started as a gymnast and trained as a dancer, but then switched to circus arts and started her own traveling circus company. Think less "tigers jumping through flaming hoops" and more "Cirque du Soleil plus roller derby." Her specialty was climbing this enormous rope that looks like anything you'd find at Home Depot. Then, when she'd climbed that rope like thirty feet in the air, she flipped upside down and hung from it by her toes.

Then she did this whole routine of spins and flips and hangs. It was pretty chill.

I interviewed Shayna at her circus's warehouse practice space in West Town, a sort of factory/meatpacking-type district in Chicago. We chatted for a bit about her background and training and then Shayna swung around on a trapeze and did a bunch of handstands and basically intimidated the shit out of me. When the interview ended, I didn't run into Shayna again until, awesomely, she and her boyfriend started coming to my stand-up shows. Hey, even a gal who hangs upside down by her toes thirty feet in the air with no net needs to laugh, and luckily, I'm so hilarious, Shayna asked me to host her circus show, and because I'm not AN IDIOT I said yes. I mean, who says no to the circus? Certainly not someone who is completely heartbroken and directionless.

Yeah, there was still an X-shaped hole in my heart, and the circus helped. We put on two shows every first Saturday and they'd always sell out. The warehouse wasn't zoned for performance so the shows were unlisted, donation-at-the-door only, and audience members entered the space by walking down a *Law & Order: SVU*–type alley of death. All of this actually helped get people out to see us—folks love an off-the-beaten-path circus. Especially when it's happening directly above them. Our several-hundred-person audience sat in the round, on the floor and in folding chairs. In the center of the circle was maybe fifteen feet of "stage"—just empty floor space.

That's where I stood, cracking wise and playing games with the audience while rigging for different acts was swapped out. Like maybe a flying trapeze act was following a flaming chain saw juggling act, and my job was to be so captivating that no one saw the trapeze scaffolding being erected right behind me. I sang songs, improvised one-liners off of audience suggestions, and did this thing where I pretended to be a "child tamer" and stuck my hand into a kid's open mouth like they were a lion. I promise that wasn't creepy. I wore welders' goggles like a headband and fancy jackets with tails and kept the show moving quickly and smoothly for two or three hours before leading a bunch of acrobats in a bow.

Then Shayna came up with the idea for a seven-city national tour—eight performers in a fourteen-passenger van for five weeks. At the Chicago shows there were men who did flips off each other's shoulders or rolled around in massive metal wheels, but the touring company was going to be all women and I was invited to be part of it. The seven acrobats were all pros and used to life on the road. They had stilt-walked in at a convention center in China or flown around on some silks (you know, those long sheets of fabric?) at a String Cheese Incident concert or taken a contract to perform at a Michael Jackson–themed Cirque du Soleil show in Vegas. I was excited to learn touring from them.

So in the fall of 2009, I threw my joke notebooks in a duffel bag and struck out on the open road with a clown, a trapeze artist, a hula hoop specialist, an acrobat who twirled on a lyra (this giant hoop), a silks performer, Shayna and her rope, and a hair-hanger, which is a person who hangs from her hair. I will call them all "the acrobats."

We started in Denver, where we slept in the same space we did shows—a tiny storefront circus studio. There was no shower, just a large kind of washing basin in the main common space. So this is where I should tell you that circus gals are really comfortable with their bodies. And they are ripped. It's pretty much six-packs, shoulder muscles, and small, perky boobs across the board. And scars. Tons of scars. It turns out that climbing a rope barefoot or gracefully dangling from a hoop by your knees doesn't feel awesome. It's painful. The rope cuts into your skin. The hoop leaves a mark. But still, onstage, your makeup has to be perfect. They didn't leave me behind there, either. I actually love makeup, but I never wear it unless someone's doing it for me because I don't know how. Bronzer makes me look like I fell in the dirt. Lipstick ends up on my forehead. But not with the circus. When an acrobat does your makeup, that shit is strong and sweatproof and that shit doesn't run.

While we were traveling through Vegas we stayed at, naturally, Circus Circus. After hours spent annoying the crap out of one another in the close quarters of the van, the distraction of a casino was exactly what we needed. We went to a buffet and I watched the gals pick out the highest-protein, lowest-carb options. Afterward, we went to the pool and the gals started showing off their skills. First one was doing a handstand. Then they all were. Then they were balancing on each other's shoulders, standing up in the pool. Two young dudes in Speedos dropped their towels, dove in, and swam out to the middle of the pool. The guys were Polish and on contract in Vegas. One dude climbed up on the other's shoulders. My gals responded with more moves of their own and soon it was a post-buffet competitive circus-off, right there at Circus Circus. The rest of the pool-goers seemed pretty impressed by the stage show. "Entertainment even in the pool!" they said. "What a full-service place!"

Each city we'd go to, we'd hook up with other circus people.

One night we stayed with some of Emily's pals—Emily was doing silks on the tour. These were folks she had met at Burning Man who made tiny top hats FOR A LIVING and owned two hairless cats and those cats were wearing some of those hats. The night we stayed with them, they were bathing crystals under the full moon to increase the crystals' potency. When you are traveling with the circus, this is the kind of situation you come to expect. Your cats have hats? Makes sense. You bathe crystals? Good!

Multiple times on tour we ended up seeking out a patch of hot springs somewhere in the desert or on an obscure island off the Washington coast, and the gals would just immediately strip down and hop in. I'd never been the strip-down-and-hop-in type, but I'd also never been in the circus. One has to be able to adapt.

One day in the middle of the tour we found ourselves in the middle of wilderness in Washington—think Forks, of sparkly-in-the-light-vampires-that-werewolves-think-smell-bad fame—and everyone decided to go skinny-dipping in a hot spring. I was sur-rounded by beautiful women and six-packs and it was essentially the makings of my own personal fantasy, except that in this real-life version I was disappointed to find that my physique hadn't transformed from a stand-up comic's body to that of a person who can climb up another person and then hang from their neck by their feet using only one million muscles that I don't think regular people are born with (this move is called a flag). I'd been around crowds of beautiful naked people before, with Allyson and X and the rest of the dancers—yes, you should be jealous—and understood that nobody cared about all the nakedness except for me. People would be casually bending all the way over with open asses and I'd just be in the corner putting on more and more sweaters. If those sweatshirts that zip over your entire face had been invented, I'd have been wearing nine.

Maybe it was just time—I was crossing into my late twenties. Maybe I'd finally gotten desensitized by years of nakedness all around me. Or maybe it was the spirit of Kristen Stewart lurking in the woods that triggered some sense of bravado within me. Whatever it was, we were in the only rain forest in North America, and I decided to just go for it. I took off all of my clothes, creating a pile that was at least double the size of everyone else's, and got into the hot spring totally naked. Immediately, one of the acrobats said, "Oh my god, you are so beautiful!" The little not-actually-fat kid inside me was surprised not just to hear that, but to realize that I believed her. "Beautiful" is not a word I associated with myself; maybe "handsome" sometimes. Never "beautiful." But the way she'd said it hadn't sounded generous or pitying or perky or feminizing, just genuine and real.

Everything about my experience with this circus was the opposite of what I'd been slogging through in stand-up. Anger and rape jokes replaced with beauty and support. They even tried to teach me some of their skills, which was a foreign thing coming from stand-up's cutthroat jockeying for spots. I learned to stilt-walk and base a two-high—which means I stood really still while an acrobat climbed up my bod and stood on my shoulders. I couldn't master juggling, that most basic of circus skills, and it turns out my tolerance for pain is more emotional than physical because they put me up on a trapeze one time and I basically cried. My tourmates were like, "Yay! You're trying!" but I gave up right away because it straight-up hurts to do that pretty shit, all slow and lean-y. The ropes cut into your hands and the trapeze is hard and gives you calluses and just FYI acrobats bleed all the time; you just can't see it from the audience. I even had a brief fling with one of my fellow travelers and it is with great pride that I can forever say: "I HAVE FUCKED A CLOWN." Thank you, the circus!

Perhaps my favorite moment happened when we were driving through Northern California.

Specifically we were in Humboldt County, where weed comes from, and our van was overheating. It was your typical hunter-green fourteen-passenger van, but packed with trapezes and glittered bodysuits, and where the back seat used to be, there was a lofted bed area for snoozing. Painted on the side of the van were the words EL CIRCO CHEAPO CABARET and this big drawing of two gals on a trapeze. So it was a circus van. We were a circus, in a circus van.

The A/C hadn't worked all day and then Shayna turned on the heater to pull heat off the engine and the van went from fairly smelly to "Oh god wow. That's too much human scent," very quickly. Sweating and cranky, the acrobats all started stripping down to their undies. Why wouldn't they? It was hot and their bodies were perfect. I waited a bit to see if things might change. Would the van get suddenly chilly and easy on the nose? Would my body suddenly become rock hard from that five minutes I'd spent crying on the trapeze?

And then, hot as fuck and nearly about to lose consciousness, I remembered something: I was beautiful. So—and you know how hard this was for me—I took my shirt off, too. They kept going, the acrobats. Some of them shed bras (some of them never wore bras to begin with) but I stopped with my shirt. I kept my shorts on, even. But it was a MOMENT. I had Adam and Mark pulling for me in Chicago and broken hearts from first love and grown-up love, my family knew my life and me, and I was funny.

That day, I didn't need a shirt.

Then we started seeing, as we continued to drive, some hitch-hiking kids. They were a certain type of hitchhiking kid that made sense for Humboldt: white dudes in their midtwenties, wearing every type of corduroy at once and carrying army surplus back-packs. The kind of kid who says, "Hey, man," and is too young to really love the Grateful Dead that much. We didn't pick any of those kids up. To this day, I still consider that such a missed opportunity. Because if you are the kind of kid who hitchhikes through Humboldt, you probably smoke a shit-ton of pot. You've probably bathed some crystals under the moonlight to increase their potency. And if you are that kind of person, and a fourteen-passenger van pulls over, flings open the door, and invites you inside to travel with a naked circus, you've got a real problem. Because that's a pretty unbelievable story and you might wear too many wales of corduroy to be considered a reliable narrator. I mourn for the fact that there isn't some young fella out there mumbling, "You gotta believe me: NAKED. CIRCUS," to his friends over goji berries and a fat joint.

I was inside that van as it rolled past. That's what sticks with me. The belonging. I've been a gay, out, shirtless ringmaster. What the fuck have you done? Oh, you're a doctor? Well, fine.

JUST FOR LAUGHS

The biggest comedy festival in the world is called Just For Laughs and it's held annually in Montreal. Imagine Comic-Con but the Starfleet is Tiffany Haddish, Trevor Noah, Amy Schumer, and Ali Wong, and the cosplayers are every talent booker or casting director or person-in-a-suit-who-makes-comedy-decisions.

For newer stand-ups, the focus of Montreal is New Faces. Each year bookers for the festival zoom around the country watching a zillion sets by a zillion emerging comics. From these auditions about twenty comics are chosen as New Faces and these baby comics make their debut at Just For Laughs with a little extra fanfare. It's like a debutante ball or a bar mitzvah, though I've never been to one of either of those. Invite me to your child's bar mitzvah!

For behoodied young comics, New Faces is a chance to meander into a party with an open bar, toss a rain forest's worth of live performance business cards in the air, and then fly back home. Being showcased at this part of the festival is an early goal I set in stand-up—probably a goal most young stand-ups share, even though it's now possible to bypass traditional systems like this and get hired or cast straight off social media.

I first auditioned for New Faces after I'd been doing stand-up for a year. My jokes were awful and I wore a white vest with hand-painted blue neon stars on it to make sure everyone got that message. I've always said, "If you're wearing a star vest and you've been doing stand-up for twelve months, you probably aren't ready to do comedy on a national level." I didn't get a callback.

The next year I sailed through two rounds of auditions in Chicago and was invited to do a final round of callbacks in New York. I flew myself out there and crashed on my college friend's Upper East Side couch. I felt great and couch-rested, and bragged to my friend, "Yeah, I'm at the level now in my career where I can afford to fly myself to audition for things I won't be paid for. Kind of a big deal." That year's vest was better—kind of argyle with a little bow tie—but the moment I walked onstage and saw the New Faces booker in the audience, I sweated through my outfit and other things I wasn't even wearing and then proceeded to eat shit for five and a half minutes. I bombed so hard that when I walked offstage, I just kept going. I walked eighty blocks from the Village back to my friend's Upper East Side couch.

It was an eighty-block-walk-level bomb.

But I kept at it. I auditioned for years, once while still wearing a hospital bracelet after a trip to the emergency room during a really bad flu. I made it through round after round, always getting cut right at the end.

The first time I played Just For Laughs it was to tape something for HBO and the second time it was to screen an episode of a television show I wrote, produced, and starred in. Now I can't stop getting booked there; I literally am there every year, remembering I don't speak French (sigh, how difficult), but I never had that New Face.

Maybe you don't, either. That's okay.

Right after I got back from my circus tour, Tig Notaro came through Chicago for a run at the now defunct Lakeshore Theater.

I opened for her and it went well enough that, a few months later, when I found out she was going to be in Austin the same weekend I was, I used the most futuristic technology available to me and sent Tig a Myspace message asking if she'd give me a five-minute guest spot during one of her shows. She gave me spots on two.

I brought the person I'd just started seeing (a roller derby–playing sweetheart) and a bunch of college pals who lived in Austin to watch me do five-minute sets. Both times I struggled to finish five minutes strong at the several-hundred-seat club—it was a much larger audience than I was used to—and both times we stayed to watch Tig's set.

In my memory, Tig killed so completely that I couldn't even laugh. My sweetheart and friends laughed their heads off—the whole audience did—but I could only stare. This was years before her album *Live*, before she appeared regularly on *This American Life* and *Conan*. I had only been doing open mics and seven- to ten-minute booked spots at the time and hadn't yet seen many comics perform a full hour.

As I watched Tig, the question "How is she doing this?" replayed again and again in my mind. It was followed by "And how do I do this?"

The way her jokes were crafted, her command over the stage, and her ability to connect so completely with the audience—I couldn't wrap my mind around any of it. We were playing the same game, but she was at boss level and I was blowing into a Nintendo cartridge to see if I could get it to work.

That's the beautiful thing about stand-up: You get to see what you are working toward. You watch comics you love from afar, then you get to open for them and then you get to work alongside them.

It never stops being cool to unlock an achievement you watched a comic ahead of you handle with ease—to grow into your career.

Of course, you don't get to see the path you'll take to get there.

Today I get that ask from newer comics: "How do I do this?" If you are a newer comic and you've asked me this question, I take it as a huge compliment. It's a vulnerable question and it makes me think you trust me.

It's something I, too, eventually asked out loud to Maria Bamford, whom I fucking love forever because she upped my pay out of her own pocket when I opened for her in Chicago and on the road. I asked her, "How do I do this?" and she patiently answered basically the same way I do now.

To do stand-up, you just begin. You get to an open mic, you tell a joke, you write a new joke, and repeat. You start your own show, invest time in getting to know your fellow comics, and you try to get a good tape of you telling jokes to send to bookers. You meet people involved in the comedy scene—producers, bookers, comics. You meet more people. You make one friend and repeat. Brick by brick, you build a little comedy house you get to live in.

Unfortunately, I've got some bad news, too. "How do I do this?" isn't really what people mean to ask. I know this because it's not what I meant, either. If you do stand-up, you already know how to do "this." You're already writing jokes, going to open mics, doing booked shows.

When I watched Tig or asked Maria those years ago, I wasn't trying to figure out how to do "this." I'd gotten booked to open for them, or asked for guest spots. I was playing the game. What I wanted wasn't help figuring out how to do stand-up; I wanted to level up, become viable, Pinocchio myself into a real comic.

I wanted to know how to do what I was watching them do. I wanted to know how to do "that."

"That" is the impetus that drives us. It's the reason any of us started doing stand-up. I think it's the reason any of us start doing anything. "That" is what we experienced watching our favorite comic live for the first time (hello again, Margaret Cho!). "That" is watching couples emerge from city hall in Boston and thinking, *Huh. I guess I could get married someday.* "That" is when I heard someone got a manager or agent or New Faces. It's the microphone-shaped carrot just out of reach.

The thing is: You never reach it. You never do "that." You might get to headline at clubs where you used to open and you might develop hours of material to replace that first five minutes you wrote, but you never get to catch up with the comics who started before you and you never get to the point where you understand what moves you'll have to make to get to the next level. The carrot always stays out of reach. Or you grab the carrot and eat it and you're like, "Fuck! I need another carrot!" Or the carrot goes mushy in your hands.

Say you get a TV show on a new streaming service and then that streaming service shuts up shop, or you write a great hour of material, record it, release it, and it's a hit. Either way you always gotta make more. There is no one success or one failure that makes you. There is no perfect joke. Goals will blow up in front of you. You'll wear the wrong vest and fail. Or wear a better vest, still fuck it up, and take an eighty-block walk.

All of this is actually good for you, but it doesn't feel good. It feels like shit. I'm not suggesting that you should play the comedy violin while the Rome of your career burns. I'm saying that every comic—every person, really, so go ahead and use this as allegory if you wanna be all *Old Man and the Sea* about it—has had this experience, because every comedy career is flush with it. If you get every New Face or Fresh Buddy or Best of 30 Under-60 Female Dog Impersonators, how will you recover when you're openly booed, or you get your own television show and then it's abruptly canceled, or your brother-in-law makes off with all the cash from your sold-out Madison Square Garden run?

Every comic I respect has failed massively, picked their shit up, and moved forward. And they'll continue to do so. It's not about getting beyond the failure; it's about outlasting it. If you hope to make comedy a lifelong career and you are lucky enough to live a long life, outlasting is the answer. Outlasting doubt, outlasting failure, and keeping a hare's short-term goals on your mind while running a tortoise's race.

Listen, maybe I don't know what the fuck I'm talking about. Maybe you'll achieve everything you set your mind to right in a row. God, you'll be insufferable. Or maybe you've already gotten knocked down and you hate me for writing a quasi-motivational Stand Up to Failure TED Talk. You can take my thoughts on this or not. I'm just saying I do actually get it—what it's like to live inside the question of how to get started or how to keep going.

I am a real human being with goals and dreams for my life. Sometimes I feel like I'm doing the damn thing and sometimes I feel like a massive disappointment. Then other times, I wish I felt plain old disappointment instead of full-on fear, hopelessness, self-doubt, and shame, especially since this job (and maybe also life) works a lot like one of those in-the-dark roller coasters where you can't see the drops. I've thought things were going great and then had my television show, network, and marriage canceled (that's another book). And I barely survived it.

Once I performed at a college in Iowa and one of the students who helped organize the show drove me back to the airport. College gigs can run the gamut, but this one had gone well. I was feeling good. The gal who was driving me was sweet and chatty and I liked her right away.

It was finals week, and she was stressed—stressed about the work she needed to finish and the different kinds of work she would need to find once she graduated. She was a senior and not sure where she wanted to live or who with or what jobs she'd even be looking for. As she talked about her life, she also asked about mine, and because she asked the questions a twenty-three-year-old would ask, I came off as a goddamned genius.

I told her about living in LA at the base of a mountain that I hike almost every day. I told her about my amazing beautiful handsome most perfect dog, Murph. I told her that I'm unbelievably lucky that I got to pick what I do for a living and that I find it fulfilling. That I don't believe in any of the specific tenets of the faith I grew up in, but that I do find comfort in some—AND ONLY SOME—of the stories it taught me. That I'm not super close with many of my exes and that it was right for us to break up eventually, but that I also think they're all cool and I'm glad we were together. I told her how I live far away from my family and I miss them and we constantly FaceTime.

Before I moved to LA, I didn't understand why anyone would willingly relocate to such a crappy, dismissive, segmented, cut-throat place where there's no sense of community or culture and the people are vain and vapid and made of cars and Botox.

Whenever I heard of anyone moving to LA, I'd imagine their convertible repeatedly stalling out à la *Romy and Michele's High School Reunion*. I saw LA as a city of dreams and "making it," and I hated the idea that anyone decided to pursue a dream with complete abandon. It just seemed so impractical. And selfish. And unhinged. I assumed cool people stayed in Chicago and dealt with threesome hecklers and fought to be discovered after coming home from their day jobs. Fuck LA, you know?

Then, a group of Chicago comics I knew and liked and respected moved to LA. Over the years, I saw them on TV or in movies or I'd catch a glimpse of their tour schedules. I started to visit LA and got up at a few shows and went to a few parties and I began to wonder if I'd been wrong. *Maybe LA is welcoming*, I thought. *Maybe there is culture and maybe the people are cool. Maybe moving to Los Angeles to pursue a dream isn't a ridiculous thing to do.*

In the years that my mind began to change, stand-up itself became less dreamy. I wasn't just open mic–ing; I was headlining local shows. I quit my day job. I started to tour. And once I got out on the road, I worried about the prospect of staying in Chicago.

I began to imagine myself at fifty, living in a city that just didn't have any jobs in my field outside of live performance and scraping rent together with live show earnings. I imagined myself having to go out every night for a set at some bar and having to drive to Milwaukee or Peoria or Madison every weekend and missing all the events my not-yet-existent kids would ever have and never sleeping in the same bed as my future partner. And I thought, *Oh, I'm gonna need to move somewhere where comedy is also a day job.*

I moved with nothing besides a very supportive then-partner. I didn't realize how much nothing, or maybe I wouldn't have gone.

No agent. No manager. No couch. No apartment. No bookings. No work. I showed up anonymously in one of the world's most anonymous cities, my full *Star Wars* Pez collection in tow, with a bit of name recognition from some LA comics I'd come up along-side in Chicago and nothing else.

And when I arrived, no one cared that I'd moved. Everyone I met was friendly and lovely and kind and working on their own shit. But they didn't care that I was there. After all, at one point or another they'd moved there with nothing, too. In LA, I wasn't shit. What surprised me was how little that ended up mattering. It's almost good to be nothing for a bit. It helped me to see the scope of the place and the duration of the commitment to the city. That commitment being: lifetime.

Because, you see, Los Angeles is about the long game. It's a city where you will work if you can survive a very slow climb and outlast confidence-shattering setbacks. People move to LA not because they have a dream, but because they have a dream they plan to achieve. It's the entertainment industry's Washington, DC, and no one gets to arrive as president and no one gets to be president forever. It's more than a city of dreams. It's a city of work, and that's a good thing. I like to work.

This student driving me to the Des Moines airport didn't ask where the fuck I was going to get kids—since there's a bit of extra planning required—or what's up with owning a house and how is that even possible? She didn't ask about marriage or divorce. She didn't ask why if I have one drink, I wake up at three o'clock in the morning to sweat and shit it out, or when we are all going to die and what regrets we'll have. She was twenty-three years old. Those are thirty-seven-year-old questions.

So I told her: "Try to relax and remain open." Followed up by: "Plan for what you want now and prepare for that to change." In other words, some really true garbage. Really true because those are two of the best things I've learned in my life so far. Garbage because I ignore those two things multiple times a day. Those things and a bunch of other acquired wisdom, too, like not to get a cabbage-based salad on a plane. I've made that mistake several times and I know it's wrong and I still might do it again.

But she didn't know about my plane salads, so as we pulled into the terminal, she said, "Wow. You've got it all figured out. I wish I could just fast-forward time to be where you are," and I let it ride, basking in nailing it for a moment before exiting her car. Then I gave her the old wink 'n' wave, threw my duffel over my shoulder, and headed into the airport like some super-chic Saint Nick.

The cinematically correct thing to do would have been to turn around at the last moment and yell out, "You can't fast-forward it! And you shouldn't try!" but I didn't, because I'm a normal person who only occasionally does cinematically correct things, like that one time I used a power loader to fight an alien.

But you and I know the truth: At twenty-three, I was living in Boston. I'd just graduated from college and was working at a high school during the day and an improv theater at night and was about to be fired. I had a girlfriend I was cheating on and wasn't yet out to many of my friends and family. I had no idea what the fuck I was doing or going to do.

Kind of like now, when I still don't. And I'm out here living the moments I planned for and those I didn't predict, hoping to someday be an Old Face, still kicking around comedy, improving set by set.

EPILOGUE

Years ago, I did a show in the well-appointed basement of a beautiful hotel on Manhattan's Lower East Side. Reggie Watts, comic and bandleader for *Late Night with James Corden*, was on the bill right before me. He wasn't yet so famous, but he was a comic's comic and a comedy nerd favorite and he crushed hearts and minds with joy during his set. I was no one in the comedy world— hadn't been on TV, wasn't touring or even headlining in Chicago.

After his set, Reggie sat down on a couch in the front row and watched me anyway.

I did well. My material worked and the energy was right. I was in sync with the audience, in sync with myself; I riffed, working in concert with the audience's vibe, incredibly present and of the moment. And I started to have this feeling like the room's low ceilings were gently pushing down against me and against the audience and that I was rooting my energy—my atoms and my parts smaller than atoms—down through the floor then up into each audience member, creating a linkage between all of us. *I'm a tree*, I thought. *My roots are reaching theirs*. We were all linked up, one organism, and it felt like I was breathing through their mouths and they were breathing through mine. The word that most comes to mind is "connected": I was connected to myself and the audience, and they were connected to me. We were one being.

Now, I had this feeling in my mind and body but I didn't speak it aloud because:

1. I was in the middle of a set and crushing.
2. I didn't want to sound unwell.

Here's where it gets trippy. When the show ended, Reggie approached me. "That was a great set," he said. "It was a real pleasure to watch you work tonight. I think my favorite part was how you were a tree, with roots going down and out to all the folks in the room."

Holy shit, right???

And now that you've read that story, you honestly don't even need to try psychedelics. Or watch *Black Mirror*. I had to put on a tie-dyed tee with a frog giving the peace sign on it just to think about and relive all this.

If I zoom out from that story, though, it feels predictable. Comedy has, in the almost twenty years since I started doing improv in college, been the way I found acceptance, new ideas, and a place in the world. It hasn't been perfect, but it's been a provider, a baseline, and a hinge. And for me, and I guess maybe also Reggie, stand-up in particular is spiritual. I wanted to follow and then *be* a priest for the first two decades of my life. I wanted the altar, the tradition, and the resolute right and wrong. But that's not what I want anymore. I don't want to be up in front of you, all brave-faced and certain. I want to be a gay-ass tree, rooted down through the floor, networked together with the queer folks and straight folks and everyone in my audience.

Stand-up brought me into a lesbian bar postshow in Nashville—the Lipstick Lounge—where I sang karaoke with a crowd of queer folks I'd have never met otherwise. Like that time I said the Hail Mary with an elder in Jamaica, the Nashville queers and I shared a common language. This time, it was Kacey Musgraves lyrics.

The day I wrote the section in this book on Improv Asylum being the only job from which I've ever been fired, I walked out of my weekly show at the Upright Citizens Brigade Theatre and ran into the former director of that theater. Hadn't seen him in fifteen years. He said he'd heard me doing press for my special *Rape Jokes* and learned for the first time what had been going on in my life while we worked together. "I wish I had known what you were going through and could have been helpful in some way," he said. I'd been honest in my special about my experiences in college, and that honesty brought kindness and healing back into my life from a pretty unlikely source.

So I'll say: I'm fucking mad at the religion I grew up in. I'm mad that Catholic doctrine still swims in my mind, that I think in Bible stories, regard Sundays as sacred, and love when radio stations start playing Christmas carols in October. If "O Holy Night" comes on while I drive past the jack-o'-lanterns still out on your porches, I will likely BLAST IT and get taken in by the comfort of the things I grew up with. It's like rewatching *Back to the Future* or *Sixteen Candles* as an adult and being like, "Wait. I think that scene/major plot point is actually sexual assault," as nostalgia turns to unsettling recognition.

Once a year or so, I wonder if I should go to church. Then I remember, "Nope!" I'd get "Don't fall for bejeweled taboos meant to preserve the wealth, power, or dominance of a few white men" tattooed on my forearm, but you can't get your first tattoo at thirty-seven.

And yet, one of the Bible's greatest hits stays with me: "God is love." (1 John 4:8) It's often interpreted as God is made of love or "God loves," but there's another interpretation: that the love between people or across a community is God.

Look: Humans are scared out of our minds and want to be saved. We want to know why we are here, what we are supposed to be doing, and how to protect ourselves. Like Dolly Parton, I am a seeker, still out here hunting down the answers to those questions. Best I can tell for now: Connection. Connection to ourselves. Connection to others.

Maybe that connection *is God*. And we're our own saviors, meant to save ourselves.

ACKNOWLEDGMENTS

First off, thank you to the "business guy" support system that made this book possible: Todd Sellers, Alex Murray, and everyone at Brillstein. Also Eve Attermann, D. C. Wade, Andrew Russell, Dave Tamaroff, and everyone at WME and Gersh at different phases of this project. Plus Maddie Caldwell, Libby Burton, and the folks at Grand Central.

Thank you, Mom, Dad, Al, and Brit! Thanks, Ben, Addie, and Chris.

Love you, Murph!

Also extremely grateful to the personal support system that had my back during the year this book was in hyperdrive. Thank you, Laura Vichick, Todd Pate, Nate Urbansky, Kelli Auerbach, Elliot Musgrave, Pony Lee Musgrave, Candy Lawrence, and Hannah Burque.

Big giant extra thank you to Katy Nishimoto.

NOTES

1. "Walk the Line," *BC Heights*, November 3, 2016, http://bcheights
   .com/magazine/index.php/2016/walking-the-line-history
   -lgbtq-community-boston-college/.
2. October 1, 1986, available online at http://www.vatican.va/
   roman_curia/congregations/cfaith/documents/rc_con_cfaith
   _doc_19861001_homosexual-persons_en.html.
3. National Institute on Drug Abuse, "Substance Use and SUDs in
   LGBT Populations," September 2017, https://www.drugabuse
   .gov/related-topics/substance-use-suds-in-lgbt-populations.